BILL & GERALDINE

INTERNATIONAL BESTSELLER

BEYOND
BROKE

BILL & GERALDINE TEGGELOVE

INTERNATIONAL BESTSELLER

BEYOND
BROKE

Recover and Flourish from Financial Meltdown

FOREWORD BY BOB PROCTOR, STAR OF *THE SECRET*

TAG Publishing, LLC
2618 S. Lipscomb
Amarillo, TX 79109
www.TAGPublishers.com

Office (806) 373-0114
Fax (806) 373-4004
info@TAGPublishers.com

ISBN: 978-1-59930-377-2

Cover: Daniela A. Savone
Text: Eric Choi

First Edition

Acknowledgements

Without our outstanding publishing team, this book would not have been possible. They are the best, and it was a pleasure to work with them. We are very grateful to our project team, Anna Sajeki, Liz Ragland and Dee Burks; they were not only a delight to work with, but were very professional in all aspects of the process.

We would like to thank and acknowledge the many people who have helped us on our journey in writing *Beyond Broke.*

Personal growth comes out of the many obstacles on our path, so we acknowledge the many people who have challenged us, some in ways they may never know. We are grateful for the growth opportunities they have provided.

Special acknowledgement must go to Geraldine's sister, Katherine, for her unwavering faith, love, and support of us in our journey over the past four years. She always knew exactly what we needed and gave unconditionally. For this, we will be forever grateful.

We have been blessed with many teachers over the years, and we would like to especially mention Anthony Robbins, Bob Proctor, and Rev. Robert Wasner. To the many authors in the field of personal development, we say thank you for your inspiration and encouragement.

Finally, we wish to acknowledge each other. We have been through tough and challenging times over the past few years, yet throughout our ordeal, our love, commitment, and admiration for each other has truly blossomed. We are true soulmates.

About the Authors

Geraldine Teggelove

Geraldine Teggelove has spent the majority of her life helping others. Now, with a Masters in Metaphysical Studies, she is fulfilling her real passion and purpose through helping people reach their full potential in life and live their dreams. As a Mentor and Spiritual Healer, she uses her skills to assist others to overcome adversity, restore self-esteem and take the necessary steps to move forward in life. In doing so, participants clarify their purpose, stay focused, maximize their unique gifts and successfully move from crisis to prosperity.

Through utilizing her vast knowledge of Meditation techniques, she teaches her clients how to restore emotional balance in their lives; replacing stress, worry and fear with peace and calm.

As a highly successful recording artist, her songs have brought healing and inspiration to many.

Bill Teggelove

After working as a Secondary School Principal, Bill realised that his talent for helping children succeed should be extended to adults as well. In 2008, Bill launched Teggelove Mentoring and Coaching. With extensive experience as a qualified Life Coach and Master Practitioner of neuro-linguistic programming (NLP), Bill uses a coaching technique centred on a clear vision for his client's future and effective goal setting methods.

As an experienced professional, Bill understands the unique needs of his clients and treats each individual with personal attention and assistance. He has coached both corporate and private clients through serious health, career and financial issues to gain a much improved quality of life. He enjoys helping others and finds many personal rewards through Teggelove Mentoring and Coaching.

This book is dedicated to the greatest teachers in our lives: our three beautiful children, Elissa, Jacinta, and Michael. They have brought out the very best in us as they have grown and matured into magnificent adults.

This book is also dedicated to everyone who dares to dream, who is open to the possibilities, has the courage to step out in faith, and who never quits.

Foreword

For well into two decades, I've worked with people to help them achieve financial success. I firmly believe that the financial path we travel down depends on our mindset. Each one of us has the potential to live a life of prosperity; it is just a matter of whether or not we believe it. Bill and Geraldine Teggelove's book, *Beyond Broke*, reaffirms the teachings in my "You Were Born Rich" program. This book guides you along their journey from financial ruin to unlimited abundance and prosperity.

I was amazed at their innate ability to help people create a climate of positive thinking that will impact their financial status. In simple terms, Bill and Geraldine detail how it is possible to transform your life by changing your mindset and living in harmony with the laws of the universe. It is just a matter of making ourselves aware of these laws and applying them to our lives. *Beyond Broke* gives you the necessary techniques to live a life without limits.

By focusing on the positives rather than dwelling on the negatives, Bill and Geraldine offer a brighter financial future. With practical knowledge and vast experience, Bill and Geraldine help those suffering from financial stress successfully manoeuvre through every stage of the recovery process. After reading *Beyond Broke*, you'll be more than prepared to work through your financial woes and flourish. I encourage you to not only read this book, but to actually apply the wisdom contained within to achieve true success as the universe intended.

—Bob Proctor

Contents

Introduction

In many ancient cultures, fire played an important role in the development of civilization. It is also one of the four classical elements in Greek philosophy and science. Far too often, fire is associated with destruction, but in reality, those flames, feared by so many, actually bring forth a renewal of life. Forest fires, for example, are viewed as catastrophic events and are suppressed as quickly as possible. But as the fire creeps along the forest floor, it clears out the undergrowth and gives the larger trees more room to spread their roots. Some trees even require the heat of the flames to open seed pods or pine cones to complete their life cycles.

Fire represents the imagination and determination that all intellectual and emotional beings have. Commonly associated with energy, assertiveness, and desire, this active force has the passion to recreate and animate life. A good example of this is the book you are reading right now.

Many of us have heard the legend of the mythological Phoenix, which overcame death and rose from the ashes as a youthful and beautiful creature, making it immortal. The name comes from the Greek word for "purple" because it is associated with fire and the sun. As the story goes, the Phoenix gathered aromatic herbs, woods, and spices from around the world to build its own funeral pyre. Sitting atop the nest, it turned to face the rays of the sun, spread its wings, and disappeared into the flames.

As the smoke lifted, the Phoenix was reborn to great power. Today, the Phoenix is associated with resurrection, immortality, and triumph over adversity. Our life story is a modern-day version of the Phoenix. This is one of the primary reasons we decided to share our journey in *Beyond Broke*. Until recently, we didn't want for anything. With both of us in the education field earning well over six figures, we traveled extensively throughout Australia and abroad, lived in a beautiful home, and owned an award-winning business. For numerous reasons we didn't understand at the time, our wonderful life crashed, and we bottomed out financially. We wondered why this was happening to us, but as time passed and we began to look at other successful people's lives, we saw that, regardless of how successful people are, they must go through pits and troughs as well as relish in the triumphs.

Looking back, we can see that in some areas, such as our health, family, and relationships, we were soaring with eagles, whilst in all areas of finance we were plummeting down into a valley. Both of us were naïve about the financial aspects of our lives, and we just couldn't understand why we were experiencing this crash. Now we realise that this was just a cycle of life we had to endure. Through our desire for personal growth, we came to the realization that the deepest of troughs gave us the strength to ascend to the highest of mountains.

By overcoming our adversity, we have breathed new life into each other and our story. So the question remains: Why is it that some who experience financial hardship are able to persist through the bad times and regain their holdings, while others can't seem to move beyond their misfortune? Unfortunately, far too many of us believe that we will never rise from the smoldering remains of our financial mistakes. As a result, those who have fallen on hard times think they are destined to remain in their current situation.

This is certainly not the case; we bottomed out financially yet managed not only to pick ourselves up and move forward, but to find and follow our dreams at an age when most people think about retirement. It is our sincere hope that as your read the pages that lie ahead, regardless of your financial situation or age, you'll be able to chart a new course for your life, soar through the sky, and share the company and freedom of eagles.

Chapter I

Rising from the Ashes: In the Beginning

The first and greatest victory is to conquer yourself;
to be conquered by yourself is of all things most shameful
and vile.

– Plato

Initially, we lived life to the full. Travel, theatre, concerts, spending time together – whatever we wanted was at our disposal. With our highly successful careers in education and educational administration, as well as owning an award-winning bed and breakfast, it seemed the world was ours for the taking. The thought of living any other way was foreign to us. We were comfortable with every aspect of our lives.

Comfort Zones

The majority of people in the world today love the familiar. They want to know what to expect every morning when they get out of bed. This isn't necessarily bad. But in life we get what we focus on, and if we spend our days wearing blinkers and looking only in the same direction, our lives aren't going to change. Let's take the example of your favourite restaurant. When you go there, do you find yourself ordering the same entrée each time? Stop for a moment and think about the last time you went shopping for new clothes. What did you buy? The same type of shoes or jeans that you just donated or threw away?

When we repeatedly live in the same manner, eating the same foods, wearing the same types of outfits, and driving the same way to and from work, the actions become unconscious and turn into habits. How many times have you started your car and, before you know it, you're sitting in the parking lot at work? Have you talked on your mobile phone while driving but made all the correct turns and made it to your destination safely? These things are done unconsciously and habitually.

Habits

We are all creatures of habit, whether we want to admit it or not. Habits are interesting in that they can be both good and bad. Healthy eating and exercising regularly are habits you want to incorporate into your life. Living blindly in the belief that nothing is ever going to change is a detrimental habit. A number of our habits hold us captive in our comfort zones rather than freeing us to reach our goals, fulfil our dreams, or just live better lives. This is primarily because habits allow you to function on autopilot.

Most habits override our ability to look at a situation from a new perspective, thus keeping us in a state of *unawareness*. Many times we don't make the conscious decisions needed to prevent a potential crisis. In our case, habits, combined with a lack of awareness, led our "perfect" lives to total collapse. We struggled with a health issue, two failing business, and the downward spiral of our investment portfolio. If your life isn't going in the direction you desire, or you are on the verge of a collapse as we were, take a look at your habits. Ask yourself, "Am I willing to continue in the same destructive pattern, or do I change my thoughts and actions?"

Change

If you took a poll and asked how most people feel about change, you'd more than likely hear answers such as "I don't like change", "I like my life just the way it is", or "Change? Why? I'm happy." Whether we realise it or not, we work very hard to stay in our comfort zones. By doing so, we feel safe and secure. Our safety lies within the walls of our comfort zones. For us, the walls of school and our bed and breakfast were more than just bricks and mortar; they were very much our comfort zone.

Inside those boundaries, life was certain and we knew what to expect, or at least we thought we did. One of our favourite phrases has now become "Expect the unexpected." How true is this? We thought we were secure, but in all reality we were very naïve in our investments and financial planning. And, truth be told, our comfort zone led us to live above our means.

To find fulfilment, we have to take a leap outside our comfort zones. As we move closer to the edges of our zones, we begin to feel a bit shaky and unsure of ourselves. But don't worry; this is normal and happens to everyone. Those edges may be jagged and painful, but they also are the place where we experience the most growth.

Watching the Sunset

Sometimes the unexpected happens. You lose a job, your home is devastated by fire, or an illness affects a loved one. Some lessons are learned the hard way. The stewardship of those lessons seems especially important. The most significant learning we experienced started with losing our financial security and having to start over.

The sunsets in our area were absolutely amazing. We lived within walking distance of the Murray River, and for me it was a magical experience to watch the sunset over the river. I spent many evenings watching the sunset during our time of crisis. As I watched the brilliant red and orange colours slowly sink into the horizon, I felt a kinship to the sunset. It became a metaphor for me and my life. I was slowing sinking, too. My life was burning away, just as the sun's energy was in the evenings. I had many long and dark nights – not just because of the lack of sun, either. The difference, however, was the sun in my life only sank; it never rose. It took me many months of self-discovery to find my sunrise.

– Geraldine

Many people don't recover from a crisis situation and never acquire the life they've dreamed about. Why is this? How can some sink into the horizon only to rise again the next day, while others can't see the light of tomorrow, next week, or next year? The answer is quite simple. They focus on the bad in their lives and don't take action. What you focus on in life is what you will receive. This holds true for both positive and negative experiences. We wasted many days focusing on our problems and financial plight, worrying about how to make ends meet, and what would happen next. It wasn't until we turned our thoughts and attention around and focused on positive outcomes that things changed for the better.

Law of Attraction

Fear is the reason so many people fail to focus. They fear the future, they fear leaving their comfort zone, and most of all they have a fear of failure. This is a never-ending cycle. You fear you won't succeed, so you don't, because that is your focus. You fear you'll fail, so you do, because that is your focus. When we look at fear as nothing more than a single word, no different than "hello", we realise the control it has over us.

The Law of Attraction states that like attracts like. This has been addressed by many people and under many different topics. It has been called positive thinking, mental science, pragmatic Christianity, new thought, science of mind, practical metaphysics, divine science, and many other terms. However, the underlying concepts are the same.

Focusing on positive energies and ideas allows positive things to be brought to you. These forces aren't subject to change and are very powerful. This law is no different than the Law of Gravity. If for example, you fall off the edge of a river bank, you don't fall up, do you? No, of course not. The Law of Gravity dictates that what goes up must come down. No matter how hard you try, it is impossible to fall up. To focus is to turn your crisis into a determined, destiny-directing goal and to passionately concentrate your creative energy on your target. But staying focused is a continuing challenge.

A multitude of distractions can siphon off your energy and drive. Disappointments and interruptions can be expected when attempting to work through a crisis. As a matter of fact, they are a part of everyday life. Even as you read this chapter, what other thoughts are passing through your mind? Is 100 per cent of your attention focused on reading this, or is your consciousness split? Is any part of your mind churning over family issues, work-related stress, or any past or upcoming events? When our minds are cluttered and we attempt to focus, it's like tossing coins into the Murray River. They don't sink to the bottom; instead, they're carried away by the currents. How many of your thoughts are carried away by the currents of distractions? How different would your life be if you could just focus?

This may be a difficult concept for you to understand. It was for us, but once we took the time to truly understand how this law works, it all began to make sense. Before reading any further, take a moment and think about your life. Are you successful and financially secure? Or are you in a constant state of worry over money? Does your life never seem to turn out the way you want? Now, relate your life back to your thoughts. Do your thoughts match your current circumstances in life? How many times have you told yourself that something bad was going to happen? You were right, but you thought the situation into existence.

How can you manifest financial prosperity when you continue to think about not having enough money to pay bills? When we tried to sell our bed and breakfast, the sale fell through two separate times. Why? Because of our focus. We were constantly asking ourselves, "What if it falls through again?" You have to build your mental discipline and your ability to stay focused on whatever you desire to achieve.

Live Consciously

Dealing with any type of a crisis situation can be a very stressful experience. As the pressure builds, you feel hopeless, as if you have nowhere to turn except on those around you. To stop this from occurring, you absolutely must take responsibility for your current situation and the events that have occurred in your life. In our coaching business, we've met hundreds of people who float through life fooling themselves into thinking that someone or something is responsible for all the bad in their lives. Unfortunately, many people never learn this important lesson, and so it stays a secret until it can be pointed out and acknowledged by an individual. Think for a minute. When was the last time you said to yourself, "I am wrong, but I can change this. I can make this different. I made a mistake, but I can change my life." Or is it always, "You need to do... He is always... They are never..."? If you find yourself constantly embracing the latter, you will never get to where you would like to be.

Taking Responsibility

You are responsible for your own life and cannot continue to blame your misfortune on others. Regardless of what happened yesterday, it happened yesterday. Leave it there! Today is going on right now, and if you are worried about yesterday's hardships while today is passing you by, you are wasting your life.

For us, we quietly blamed each other for the bad events in our lives. This contributed to our own personal stress. If only we had just taken a step back and realised that our situation was no one's fault. The moment we acknowledged and accepted this fact, our lives improved markedly. In any crisis, it is important to take control of the situation before it takes control of you.

One of the important methods to effectively deal with a crisis is to try and keep hope alive, even when it seems there is no hope left. Stress and anguish usually accompany people through a crisis, especially after they relinquish hope. Once this happens, it is difficult to handle the crisis and the circumstances surrounding it. Inevitably, additional problems arise. To successfully work through any crisis, focus on the positives.

Taking responsibility is one of the important ways we accept the givens of life. It is much easier to take responsibility in situations where we are clearly at fault, where our culpability is readily apparent. At the other extreme, it would be much more difficult, if not illogical or even impossible, to take responsibility for something that we had no direct part in. Or would it? Is it actually possible to take responsibility for negative circumstances in which we played no direct part? Throughout our lives, we are confronted with demanding situations. It isn't the circumstances that determine what we accomplish in life. Instead, it is how we handle them. People who take responsibility and see their own weakness as it relates to the problem are the people who grow and accomplish their goals. Those who blame others or ignore the pressures stagnate and achieve less.

When you take responsibility, life becomes yours. You make it what you want. Success is inevitable. On the other hand, if you fail to take responsibility and you blame others for your problems, you will be stuck in a never-ending cycle of let-downs, failures, and unhappiness. When you're faced with difficult situations in life, you have two choices in the way you respond. This goes back to the question of whether you are an optimist or pessimist. Do you face the problem positively or negatively? Those who respond positively, who take responsibility rather than blaming others or being indifferent, grow as individuals. They set the stage for great positive responses from life; they achieve and are happy. People who respond in negative ways get negative results.

By taking responsibility, we acknowledge the principle that we can change any negative outside ourselves by discovering and changing a corresponding trait within ourselves, no matter how subtle or obscure. When we shift the problem inward, the problem outside ourselves can instantaneously dissolve. By taking this approach, we can literally right the wrong that crosses our field of awareness. In that way, we can literally change the problems of the world from within. The most important lesson any human being can learn is: *Your life is yours; you and only you can make it worth living.* You are the only one who can transform your life into the life you dream of. What happened in the past is over.

Making Decisions

Once you've accepted responsibility, you're able to make conscious decisions about what needs to be done to get your life back on track. Decision making is a primary function of life, and we need to be able to make effective decisions in all areas of our lives. You need to ask yourself three questions before making any decisions.

- What type of information do I need to make this decision?

- What are the possible consequences of any decision I may make?

- How can I minimize any negative outcomes?

Decision making, then, becomes the process of making a choice based on available information, alternatives presented, values held, and intended outcomes. It is also influenced by the choices available and the way you make the decision. Once you've asked yourself the three previous questions, you are ready to take things further by:

- Identifying the problem

- Determining the desired outcome

- Creating possible alternatives

- Evaluating those alternatives

- Making the decision

- Following up on the outcomes

Some decisions are considered routine, whereas others require careful thought and consideration. Only in emergency situations do decisions have to be made immediately.

As you face the future, be prepared to make your most important decisions as if there were no tomorrow. Let us ask you this question: What would you do if you knew the world would end tomorrow? Live your life based on that answer. Don't live on assumptions or preconceived notions. Virtually every decision we make includes assumptions, known or unknown, conscious or unconscious, constructive or destructive, positive or negative.

We assume that our car will start every time. We assume that the restaurant will have our favourite dish. We assume that the people around us will be here tomorrow. More than we are aware, our opinions, judgments, decisions, interpretations, perceptions, conclusions, and resolution of conflicts are all based on assumptions, and you know what happens when you assume.

What are assumptions? They are mental observations presumed to be facts before they can be proven to be absolute reality. To make an assumption is to accept something as the truth before all sources can be traced and verified. It is committing to a viewpoint before all questions can be answered beyond a shadow of a doubt. If we were to observe and recognize all the assumptions that we make in our private, public, social, and philosophical behaviours, our limited and fragile systems would collapse under the emotional and mental overload.

To live a truly fulfilled life, you must rise above any challenge or crisis. Even though we incurred massive debts, we made the decision to pay them off rather than declare bankruptcy (which was a real option for us). In the following 12 months, we bottomed out financially. Through all of this, our dream of serving others through coaching and mentoring remained compelling.

Our life story is a modern-day version of the Phoenix. This mythical bird overcame death and rose from the ashes as a youthful and beautiful creature. By overcoming our adversity, we too have risen out of the ashes and breathed new life into each other and our story. Remember, many of yesterday's impossibilities are possible today. Many of yesterday's "facts" have been disproved. Live as if there were no tomorrow.

Chapter Questions

1. Within your crisis, what factors have you blamed on other people or circumstances?

2. What habits do you have, in relation to your crisis, that do not serve you well?

3. What decision do you need to make right now to help you move on?

4. Make a list of the ways in which your current crisis is affecting you.

Chapter II

The F.L.I.G.H.T Plan Program:
Taking Care of Practicalities

The art is not in making money, but in keeping it.

– Proverb

Many of us believe that our financial mistakes will continue to haunt us. Far too often, those who have fallen on hard times think they are destined to remain there. This is certainly not the case; we bottomed out financially, yet managed to pick ourselves up and move forward. So the question remains: Why is it that some who experience financial hardship are able to persist through the bad times and regain their holdings, while others can't seem to move beyond their misfortune?

As we looked over the edge of the cliff and watched our financial situation burn at the bottom of the valley, we knew that we had to make some vital decisions. Did we want to sit and wallow, or make the decision to move forward? As Richard Branson writes in his book *Let's Not Screw It, Let's Just Do It*, "Take that first step. There will be many challenges. You might get a few knock-backs– but in the end, you will make it."

In every aspect in life, not just financial chaos, if you want to live effectively, you need to be able to make good decisions. If you can learn to do this in a timely and well-considered way, then you can achieve spectacular and well-deserved success. However, if you dither or make poor decisions, you risk staying in a holding pattern, and failure lurks around the corner.

Decision making is more than just deciding to act; it also involves strategic planning. One of our favourite books is you^2 by Price Pritchett. In the Introduction, he describes the time he was watching a fly attempt to escape through a window. With each failed attempt to fly through the window, it was losing strength and further dooming itself to death. All this time, there was an open door only ten feet away that the fly could have easily flown through to the outside it so desperately wanted to reach.

Often when we don't reach the level of success we want, it isn't because we didn't make decisions, but because we did not make good decisions. Planning allows you to make decisions on your terms and gives you time to consider several options without the last-minute rush. This action plan is a perfect example of the Pareto principle – the idea that by doing 20 per cent of the work, you can generate 80 per cent of the advantage of doing the entire job. Pareto analysis is a formal technique for finding the changes that will give the biggest benefits. It is useful where many possible courses of action are competing for your attention. Before you make any decisions about your financial future, consider the following:

- Do your decisions give you the freedom to set the goals you want? In any decision, keep in mind that you should only focus on events that relate to your goals. Many decisions are incorrectly based on emotion or others' opinions rather than on the best course of action.

- With each decision, can you measure your success? This is important because it can show you immediately when you are off course and need to make adjustments and corrections.

- Do your decisions take into account the resources you need? Good decisions and smart planning help you maximize the resources you have. Remember that dollars are not your only resource. Mentors, books, and seminars also helped us through our difficulty and taught us valuable lessons.

- Give yourself permission to re-evaluate your decisions. No decision is set in stone. By reviewing your progress periodically, you can see concerns before they become problems, and you can shift available resources to cover the unexpected issues.

F.L.I.G.H.T Plan Program

Events such as illness, disability, employment changes, and investment failures can be as detrimental to your personal and financial well-being as they were to ours. An assessment of your situation can help define your present financial status as well as prepare for future planning, saving, spending, and dealing with financial emergencies. As we discussed options for recovering from our own financial crash, we knew that we needed to devise a plan that would help us get our lives back in order.

In keeping with the theme of our modern-day version of the story of the Phoenix, we devised the F.L.I.G.H.T Plan Program –

a six-point, fast-track action plan that lifted us from our negative situation and placed us on the runway to success.

F: Figure

L: Learn

I: Initiate

G: Generate

H: Harness

T: Thought

The techniques in this plan will help you to make the best decisions possible with the information you have available. They'll help you map out the likely consequences of decisions, work out the importance of your own individual factors, and choose your best course of action.

FIGURE:

1. Figure out where you are right now financially.

Before you can do anything, your first *must* is to figure out where you are financially. This assessment involves identifying your current financial situation, then finding a professional mentor to assist with an immediate financial plan. This includes evaluating the changes needed in order for you to reach your goals. This can be the most difficult step for most people because once they see the reality of their finances, they know they have to make changes. As we mentioned in the previous chapter, change brings out fear, and at times we would rather stagnate in our current circumstances than face our fears.

I didn't want to look at our situation on paper. I avoided this constantly. I suppose I knew on a subconscious level how badly off we were financially, but I just didn't want to have to admit it.

– Bill

Your assessment and planning should take into account your current and projected income, including wages and other earnings such as child and spousal support. Then, compare that to your present and expected costs, such as mortgage or rent, food, rates, insurance, utilities, and medical, transportation, and clothing expenses.

As you figure out your current situation, it is important to also consider the possibility of future emergencies and how to prepare for them. If you identify any financial concerns, then short-term and long-term planning, along with saving and reduction in spending, will be needed.

Visit our website at www.flightplanprogram.com for a free download of a pro-forma for accurately determining your current financial situation.

2. Figure out where you want to be financially in the months and years ahead.

This process is detailed in our discussion on moving from point "A" to point "B", outlined in Chapter V "An Inspired Vision of the Future."

3. Figure out what got you into this financial situation and what may stop you from moving forward into prosperity and abundance.

These are really important issues for you to consider. It may seem as if your financial crisis has come upon you rather suddenly, but this is certainly not the case. What you will come to read and learn about in the remaining chapters will assist you in understanding that this has been a long time coming – it began well before the evidence was apparent.

Therefore, briefly reflecting on these issues now will begin the process of clearing the way to beginning to think at a level deeper than that which is supported by the physical evidence. Then, bit by bit, the answers will come. We also strongly suggest that you openly and honestly answer the questions at the end of every chapter to complete this process.

LEARN:

1. Learn from others.

Learning from experts is a *must*. As we began to recover from our financial meltdown, we had mentors to help us through particular issues. We had a financial planner, an accountant, and a banker. For us, our egos were the primary roadblock to asking for help. This is true for most individuals. We want help and know that we need it; the problem is that asking for and getting help is embarrassing and difficult. Sometimes we have to swallow our pride. We didn't want to have to ask for help, but we knew that if we were to survive this mess, the assistance and advice of others was paramount.

Learning is about seeking advice and applying it appropriately. It is important that the advice comes from the right people – those with the expertise to assist with particular areas of your life. Learning from mentors will be referred to frequently throughout this book.

2. Learn from the situation in which you find yourself.

Too often, when we are faced with a difficulty in life, we immediately look for a solution and move on without learning from the situation. We look for the quick fix instead of taking the time to ask ourselves, "What is the cause of this?" or "How can I do things differently so that the same problem does not recur?" It's like constantly taking pain-killers for an ailment without finding and fixing the cause. If we do not address the cause of our financial woes, the difficulties will keep occurring. Every successful person will tell you that they "failed forward" in that they constantly took risks, made mistakes, and learned the lessons.

3. Learn to look at the big picture.

The big picture starts to unfold as we *figure* out where we want to be financially in the months and years ahead. As we look at the current situation in light of the big picture, we *learn* that there is good in everything – even in adversity. You will find that looking for the good opens doors and presents new opportunities for you, if you are prepared to take action.

When I started to look for the good in our crisis, I couldn't see a thing. However, my mentor encouraged me to look for the hidden possibilities by brainstorming all thoughts, feelings, and emotions, both in the negative and in the positive aspects of my situation. To make a long story short, I am now realising a childhood dream of composing and recording my own inspirational songs.

– Geraldine

INITIATE:

1. Initiate communication.

Keeping the lines of communication open with your creditors is a *must*. Constant phone calls from collection agencies and credit card companies are among the worst aspects of being deeply in debt. Instead of waiting for them to call for payment, we found that initiating the communication and attempting to work out some sort of payment plan helped not only our mental strife, but also assisted in maintaining our good credit rating. Our experience has been that creditors are happy to work with you so long as you keep them informed and make some progress in repaying the debt.

Bob Proctor, in his book *You Were Born Rich*, detailed a debt-reduction plan and a letter to creditors, which we adapted to our own situation. The following is an example of a letter we sent to all our creditors.

{your address}

{date}

Attention: Credit Department /Collections

{name of bank or credit supplier}

{their address}

To whom it may concern,

Re: Account number / Card number {write in card number}

As you know, I am in debt to you for ${amount of debt}, as per statement dated {date of last statement}, and I intend to pay you in full, including all interest. In order to achieve this goal, I have been devising a plan (in consultation with a financial planner) during the past two weeks to put myself in a stable financial position. To this end, I have opened a "Debt Clearance Account" (DCA), and 20 per cent of my income is going directly into that account. That will enable me to have sufficient resources to live on, without worry or stress, and it will prevent me from falling further into debt.

Each month from {next month} through {suggest six months later}, you will receive a cheque for ${nominal amount} from my DCA. This will be dispatched to reach you by the 20th of each month. As from {month after final date}, I will pay you, by cheque, at the very least, the minimum monthly payment as detailed in your monthly statements, until my account with you is clear. I will be in a position to do this because my expanding business will be giving me a higher income at this time.

I attach a cheque for $100 with this letter, as payment for {current month}. This is all that I can manage immediately and will enable me to set up my debt-reduction program as indicated.

I am aware that the amount I will pay each month until {seven months from now} is not the figure I had previously agreed to pay you (as per the terms of my card application), but I am sure that you will be understanding and appreciate what I am doing.

I am also aware that the balance owed to you is above my credit limit. I am not in a position to pay the over-limit amount at this point in time, and I request you leave the balance as it currently stands until after {seven months from now}, when my finances will be in a better position. I also request that, in understanding and appreciation of what I am doing, you will not charge me any over-limit or late payment fees. I undertake not to use my card during this period of time.

If you have any questions, please feel free to contact me. I am quite excited about my new plans, and if you would like to have me review them with you so that you might be able to help others who are in debt to you, I would be pleased to do so.

Thank you in advance for your kind cooperation.

Yours sincerely,
{sign your name}
{print your name}

A template of this letter is available for you to use and can be accessed in the download section at www.flightplanprogram.com.

2. Initiate mentorship.

We have already mentioned the importance of having mentors who can assist and guide you through your recovery and on to a life of prosperity and fulfilment. Now it's time to take action. Regardless of how uncomfortable you feel, make a decision to speak to an appropriate specialist today. As with us, you will immediately have a huge weight seemingly lifted from your shoulders.

GENERATE:

1. Generate income.

Generating income wherever and however you can is a *must* if you wish to move out of your financial crisis. Adding cash flow and setting up multiple sources of income helped us improve our situation and pay off our debt quickly.

2. Generate income through employment or additional employment.

In times of financial crisis, you have to be prepared to do whatever needs to be done. Again, this can be challenging to your ego. If you're a top-level executive with good standing in the community, it can be a bit humbling to accept a position in a factory.

I worked in the field of education as a principal and an administrator, so I believed that finding a teaching position would be easy. To my surprise, I couldn't find work. So I did what I had to do to put food on the table. I took a job working the night shift at an automobile parts manufacturing plant. I learned a good deal during this time and actually came to appreciate the job and the people. My big eureka moment was having to ask to go to the bathroom during work hours. I had to let go of my ego and accept these conditions in order to do what needed to be done to support my family.

– Bill

3. Generate income through a garage sale.

We raised many dollars in selling off goods we no longer required. This generated extra, much-needed money to pay off debts. What have you got in your garage or in other storage areas of your home, including your wardrobes?

4. Generate income through the Internet.

The eBay site is a multimillion-dollar community superstore. Whilst many people have attempted to make money from eBay sales and have given up, the opportunities are there for the taking. But this may require education from a person skilled in the field. Also, eBay is evolving, and there are now new ways for anyone to *generate* an income. We are not overly tech-savvy, but through mentorship we were able to *learn* the necessary skills and techniques to succeed.

Affiliate programs are another way of producing an income via the Internet. These are available in a multitude of different areas; you just need to Google. Technologies such as Facebook and Twitter offer more opportunities, through social networks, to create a market for your Internet ventures.

5. Generate income through network marketing.

Along with our additional jobs, we were searching for a business in which we could make extra money, but the cost of entry had to be extremely low. We became involved with network marketing. This is an amazing way of producing more income. Best of all, you can decide how much money you earn, as well as how much time you are willing to invest. In the *learn* stage of our F.L.I.G.H.T Plan Program, we discussed finding mentors. When you have three dollars in your bank account, it can be a bit intimidating to search for a millionaire who is willing to mentor you. Network marketing exposed us to numerous highly successful entrepreneurs who were willing to share their strategies and help us succeed.

Robert Kiyosaki is the author of several number-one bestsellers worldwide, including *Rich Dad, Poor Dad*. In his book *The Business School*, he talks about network marketing. He states, "If you are willing to … learn and study at your own pace, the business will continue to stick by your side. Many network marketing companies are truly equal opportunity businesses. If you will invest the time and effort, so will they."

Anyone can be successful because we all come into network marketing on equal terms. We were treated with respect in a very uplifting and encouraging atmosphere. Other benefits we found through network marketing included access to low-cost personal and professional development, and association with a team of people with a very positive outlook on life. Kiyosaki goes on to say, "What I see are the real values of a network marketing business – values that go beyond just the potential of making a lot of money. I finally found a business with a heart."

HARNESS:

1. Harness by creating a budget – yes, we said *budget!*

Another *must* is to use the information you gained through the previous steps and create a budget to make plans for future spending and saving. This allows you to harness your resources. "Budget" was a word foreign to our daily use of language. We loved to eat at fine restaurants after the theatre. After a long day, it was easier to grab some take-away food than going home to cook. These were luxuries we had to temporarily give up. Each time we were tempted, we would ask ourselves, "Is this meal worth setting us back financially?" The answer was always no. By getting rid of costly habits, we could save that extra money or apply it toward our debt.

2. Harness by creating a savings plan.

We also made the decision to pay ourselves first. By this we mean putting 10 per cent of our money into savings before we paid our bills. In the past, our mindset was to pay all of the monthly expenses and then put money back at the end of the month. Well, when that time came around, we had not only paid our bills, we had spent money on cappuccinos, theatre tickets, and other "necessities". There was nothing left for savings.

I used to spend over a hundred dollars a month at the hairdresser. I remember when Bill and I first began to cut out expenses; I bought a box of hair colour at the supermarket. My sister came over and helped me dye my hair. I felt so defeated and wondered what our lives had become. But as we pulled ourselves out of the mess, I realised how much more it meant to me to be financially free than to sit for two hours in a stylist's chair. Now Bill is my colour technician, and I wouldn't have it any other way whilst we are still in this stage of rebuilding wealth.

– Geraldine

As we saw the dollars accumulate in our account, we felt confident and financially secure. Also, we developed a reward system for our accomplishments. Every time we met a goal, we treated ourselves to something small, like ice cream.

We took the opportunity to use what we learned to finally teach our own children the benefits of saving. This was something we had never done when they were growing up. Our daughter Jacinta really took this learning to heart and has been amazed at how she has been able to build a sizeable bank account in a short period of time.

3. Harness by creating investments.

As your savings grow, look at ways of moving them from a bank account, paying little or low interest, to some form of investment which will give a greater return. This can be through shares, property, or other asset purchases. For us, having lost all of our shares and property, we initially approached investing again with some trepidation. But as we came to *learn* from our mentors and the courses we undertook – many of them free – we discovered an incredibly safe way to invest in the stock market. If only we had known!

An Austrailan stockbroking and investment firm, JB Global Investment Services, has developed and implemented an investment strategy since 2004 where your shares are insured. That's right, insurance on your shares! In the 2008 market collapse, where investors lost between 40 per cent and 60 per cent of the value of their share investment including superannuation, those invested with insurance through JB Global had the majority of their investment protected. By having insurance on our shares we can confidently invest in the share market with the peace of mind knowing that if the market falls our life time savings, including superannuation, will not be adversely affected. Yet if the stock market increases we can make high profits.

One of the other main reasons why we chose JB Global was that they are the only company in Australia to link their fees to performance. If we do not make money following their advice we pay them nothing. When we make money following their advice they charge a 10% performance fee. This fee structure ensures their interests are directly correlated to ours. We have learnt that the best person to back is one who is motivated by self interest. If they are wrong and the shares they recommend go down, we have insurance – and we are not out of pocket with having to pay fees!

Further information about JB Global can be found at the back of this book.

As this book goes to print, we have recently made our second venture back into the share market. How excited we were a few short months ago when we were able to put our savings into investments and once again start our investment portfolio. This time we'll do it right!

– Bill

THOUGHT:

1. Thoughts are linked to mindset.

Education, status, or financial savvy have no bearing on whether or not you're able to recover from a loss. Your mindset is the single most important aspect that will enable you to move beyond financial chaos. The amount of money you have is directly related to your beliefs about money. A lot of people believe there is not enough money, and their lives reflect that belief. Every time you spend money, what feelings do you have? Do you feel good, or do you feel worried? What thoughts run through your head? Are you putting your happiness on hold until you have more money? Do you worry that you shouldn't be spending your money because you are thinking how much you don't have?

2. Thoughts are linked to beliefs.

As you change your beliefs about money, it will change its experience with you. Have you ever wondered about the difference between being poor and being broke? Many would say that the two are the same. We disagree. They are, in all reality, quite different. *Broke* is temporary, while *poor* is a mindset. Let's take a look at Donald Trump. He has not only become infamous for telling would-be business moguls, "You're fired!" He is also recognized for the number of times he's gone broke and then become rich again. Whether he loses his casinos, hotels, or luxury real estate, Donald rebounds to be more successful than before. This is because of his mindset.

Now let's look at an example on the other end of the spectrum. How many times have you heard about the lottery winner who becomes destitute? There are numerous stories from across the globe about the "lucky" ones who won millions of dollars only to find themselves broke less than a year later. In his book, *10-Minute Toughness*, Jason Selk notes that approximately 80 per cent of major lottery winners file bankruptcy within five years. Why is this? A mindset of lack is responsible for our financial difficulties. Those who work their way up from the bottom or build their own wealth, however easily, have the one thing that most of us lack: a million-dollar mindset. All wealth begins with it, and all wealth is maintained by cultivating this mindset of prosperity.

It doesn't matter how much money you make; if you have a mindset of being poor, you're eventually going to travel down that road. Our mindset is affected by the past, because the decisions of the past have led to the circumstances of the present moment. Every decision we have ever made, from the jobs we have taken to the investments we have made, all lead to the present moment. Everything in our past has created every aspect of our present mindset.

Unfortunately, many people believe that the past is set in stone, which makes it difficult for them to let go of their present financial mindsets. One of the most important lessons we want you to learn from this book is that the past is completely gone and cannot be changed. Your past influences, conditioning, ideas, thoughts, and decisions, dictate and decide whether you have a mindset of *broke* or a mindset of *poor*.

However, your mindset, derived from past decisions, can be changed. Whatever mindset you have as a result of the events in your life, it can be transformed. Did you grow up in a household where money was a constant struggle and the idea of never having enough hung in the air every day? Perhaps your parents' business attempt failed, and you watched them get up each morning and go to jobs they despised. Or did you live in an environment where obstacles were viewed as opportunities for prosperity? Our mindset determines the decisions we make for our financial futures. It is only when you shift to a mindset of abundance that you'll be able to move beyond any setback in life.

So the million-dollar question (pardon the pun) is: How do you go about creating this mindset? Let's try a simple exercise. In the space below, write down nine items that you would love to have.

1.

2.

3.

4.

5.

6.

7.

8.

9.

As you wrote your list, you obviously realised that you don't have these items. This creates a sense of need or want. The key is replacing this feeling of want with the sense of already having wealth. When we do this, amazing things start to occur within our brains. We must release any negative emotions and replace them with positive ones. Fill your mind with the images of the things you want, and picture yourself already having them. We discussed habits in the last chapter. The sooner you get into the habit of seeing yourself as financially sound, the sooner it will become reality.

The Osmond family is another good example of the broke-versus-poor mindset. In 1976, the *Donny & Marie* variety show debuted. By the show's second season, George Osmond, the family patriarch, wanted to raise his children in a more wholesome environment, so he built a $2.5 million recording studio in their hometown of Orem, Utah. Once the show went off the air in 1979, the family's fortunes suffered. The recording studio failed to work as a long-term venture, leaving the Osmonds facing bankruptcy.

Unlike Donald Trump, who voluntarily filed for bankruptcy, George Osmond believed differently regarding his debts. Against the advice of his attorneys, he vowed to take responsibility and pay off the debt. The family auctioned everything, including the studio and their private jets, and went back on tour to earn money to repay creditors. The Osmonds' story resonates with us. We too believe in the importance of accepting responsibility for our financial situation. In our time of bottoming out, we decided to work our way out of debt rather than shifting our burden to our creditors.

3. Thoughts are linked to habits.

Just as your mindset relates to your past, every one of your habits is connected to your perceptions of the past. This is true not just when you are engaging in the habit, but also during every thought and behaviour that leads up to it. For example, if your habit up until now has been to avoid creditors' phone calls when you feel stress or anxiety about your financial situation, stop for a moment and ask yourself if this is contributing to any of your current problems.

The best method to change your habits is to become aware of the reason for that particular action, and aware of the consequences for you and your wallet. You will then be very conscious of choosing to take the action and, with a little more trial and error and living with the consequences, you will consciously choose to change that habit. This awareness makes changing your habit or action very easy. You can always go back to your old habit and test it out, but the consequences won't change. If you choose at any time to go back to the habit or action because it used to comfort you, you will be disappointed. This is because the changes in your level of awareness have unconsciously changed your expectations; hence, the action no longer seems so attractive.

If you try to change everything all at once, it may seem too hard to maintain. But if you group items by their consequences, you may feel it is logical to replace a bad group's consequences with a good group's consequences. For example, perhaps you have a tendency to only pay the minimum payment on your credit cards. Decide to double your payment on one card for that month. And the next month, double the payment again. Soon, the decrease in your balance will become evidence enough, and you will then start to make a choice as to how to cut back on other expenses in order to allow you to have the extra money to make additional payments.

Once you're comfortable with this change, you can then move on to something else. As you implement these modifications one at a time, they become easier and eventually effortless. Don't change anything else about any other credit cards until you feel totally comfortable about your first adjustment. Then move on to your other credit cards, one at a time. When you've adjusted to your payment plan, you can then work toward eliminating all of your credit card debt forever. Making these small changes eases you into a healthy financial state.

Fiscal Fitness

Financial strife is one of the most stressful and overwhelming experiences you will face in your lifetime. Debt and a lack of money can easily cause stress to the mind and body. When you do not have enough money and/or have debt, it is a heavy emotional burden that you carry every day. This emotional burden taxes the body and adds to poor health.

Financial stress is linked to health problems like depression and sleep problems. With the rising cost of petrol and food, the mortgage crisis, and the new bank troubles we've recently seen, many of us are feeling the crunch of financial stress. Eating nutritionally balanced meals, eating natural foods, shunning cigarettes and excessive drink, avoiding stress, and getting sufficient rest and a significant amount of aerobic exercise will automatically ward off most illness and give us longer, healthier, and happier lives.

The obvious benefits of living a healthy lifestyle are direct: avoiding disease, feeling better, having more energy, and enjoying life without the burden of painful or damaging symptoms. But there are also many secondary or more indirect benefits of maintaining good health. Becoming a disciple of maintaining a healthy lifestyle can help you focus more on keeping your fiscal fitness in order as well. When your mind is fresh and you feel good, you have the energy to confront your financial issues. Also, your mind is free to develop innovative and creative sources of additional income and solutions to help you get back on track. Changing your experience with money to having more than enough, paying off debts, and having more hope supports the mind and body in maintaining good health.

Chapter Questions

1. What is your current mindset about money?

2. How has your past affected your current financial status?

3. Are the decisions you make about money based on the reality of the situation?

4. Are you willing to sit down and look at all aspects of the F.L.I.G.H.T Plan Program with an open mind?

5. How do your financial habits affect your life?

6. Does your health contribute to your financial status?

Chapter III

Why Am I Here? What's My Life's Purpose?

There is one quality which one must possess to win, and that is definiteness of purpose, the knowledge of what one wants, and a burning desire to possess it.

– Napoleon Hill

Have you ever had one of those days where you just feel off? You are standing in front of the mirror just waiting to receive some divine guidance to know exactly what you should be doing with your life. As you stare at yourself, you think, "Is this all there is?"

What is the biggest reason most people don't get the results they want in their personal and professional lives? They don't have purpose and an unwavering commitment. Did you know that half of all businesses fail within the first two years, and 90 per cent fail within the first five years? Why is that? We believe that most of these businesses were started with one intent – to make money.

From our experiences, we know firsthand that going into an entrepreneurial endeavour just for the money is a horrible mistake. If you don't absolutely love what you're doing, then it will eventually become just another job. Living without knowing your purpose feels like an eternity of bad Monday mornings. Now more than ever, you must slow down and take the time to know your own specific purpose and what you were put on this earth to do.

So many people live their lives every day without thinking about purpose, and they appear to do just fine. You can stay busy 24 hours a day, manage your family, career, and life's obligations for the next 50 years, and not move your purpose in life forward. This is like going to a concert and not being able to hear the music. It is like walking around as an unfulfilled, empty person who goes through the motions without knowing what true happiness is. Living your purpose brings a deep passion and joy that is yours for the taking when you focus your time and energy on vision.

Life is about purpose, faith, belief, joy, and integrity. It doesn't matter if you groom dogs or trade stocks for a living – if you don't have a genuine desire for what you're doing, it will be nearly impossible to obtain success and live the life you have always wanted. Sure, you may make money, but that success is external. How happy are you on the inside? A mansion on a hill, a garage full of luxury sports cars, and a hearty bank account can't bring you peace and contentment. Money should only be a by-product of business. With a foundation built on purpose, your results will be greater than you ever imagined possible.

There is at least one aspect of our lives that we care deeply about, and each of us is good at some sort of activity. We were each given our own individual talents and abilities by a divine force. The universe has a plan for us, and part of that plan is to fulfil our purpose. We were built specifically for our purpose in life. We know from experience that we become fulfilled as people when we act to become who the universe planned for us to be. Pilots need a flight plan before they can take off and land safely at their final destination. Our lives are no different. How can we try to build our lives without first consulting our own personal plans?

So how are your results? Are they what you want? After reading the above paragraph, are your actions based on the wrong reasons? Does your business or career clash with your beliefs and integrity? Have you strayed off the path to your purpose? Or are you still searching for it? Whether you know your purpose or not, you need to ask yourself one question on a daily basis. Right now, before reading any further, ask yourself, "If I knew I was going to die tomorrow, what would I do right now?" Some may think this is a rather morbid thought, but in all reality it helps to focus your mind on the right priorities.

A few years ago, we stopped asking ourselves what we wanted to do with our lives. Instead, we started asking what we were passionate about. Soon we discovered that our passions weren't in education administration or running a bed and breakfast. When we took an open and honest look at our lives, we knew that we wanted to be a positive influence for others in a different setting. For us, our desire to help others achieve their dreams led to the creation of our coaching and mentoring business. Take an open and honest look at your life and how you feel about yourself. Do you jump out of bed in the morning, or do you hit the snooze button ten times so you don't have to face the day? Is it time for you to uncover or rediscover your passion in life? Knowing our purpose in life helps us to focus our energies. When you focus your energies toward your destiny, you will find greater fulfilment because you are acting according to your divine creation. Once you find this fulfilment, you'll find the results you've been missing.

Your Values Shape Your Destiny

Your decisions should be based upon not only your purpose, but your values as well. It makes sense, since your values are woven throughout your life's purpose and goals. They serve as your compass to guide you through financial problems and any other of life's storms that blow your way. When faced with a decision that contradicts your personal values, choose to stand up for what you believe rather than disregard and dishonour your values. Decisions based fundamentally on core values, as well as process outcome, will be those that foster creative thoughts and ultimately lead toward success.

We experience emotional discomfort when acting outside our values systems because we aren't in alignment with our true selves. Our actions don't reflect our thoughts. This makes us feel insecure, have poor self-esteem, and doubt ourselves – hence the discomfort. For this reason, our values should always be a guidepost for our behaviour. Keep in mind that your actions show yourself and the world what is important to you. If, for example, you believe that giving is an important aspect of life, yet you don't offer up any portion of your finances, is giving really one of your values? Ask yourself what outsiders would think if they looked at your life as a case study. What would they think your values are? When you choose to ignore your values, you choose a path away from your authentic self, and you don't fulfil your destiny.

Accomplishing Your Purpose

Many of us are very good at making plans, but we lack the ability to execute. We stick our heads in the sand, more than likely out of fear, never realizing how powerful we can become if we continually work towards our purpose in life. How about you? What should you be doing to follow your passion? Do you really want to make a major difference in this world, or are you just willing to make a small contribution in your local community? Positive change doesn't just happen. You must take specific, disciplined action. Now let us warn you that this action is often uncomfortable. Any time we venture into the unknown, we tend to feel a bit suffocated. So ask yourself if you're willing to step out of your comfort zone.

Once you decide to pursue your purpose, how do you stay motivated? First of all, you need to realise that you are making a significant investment in your life. For example, if you bought a new car, you wouldn't leave it parked outside with the keys in the ignition. No, instead you would keep it in the garage with the door down. So many people fail to view themselves as an investment. Program your mind to be positive all the time. We began with books, cassettes, and seminars. Today there are CDs, DVDs, iPods, and online resources. They are all just a phone call or click of the mouse away. For you to realise how important *you* are, it is imperative to install good programming into your mind to overcome years of negative programming.

Remember, nothing happens if you don't act. You can't improve by wishing. You don't live the life you've always wanted by sitting on the couch and eating potato chips. Think about where you want to go, and stay away from those who drain your energy and bring you down to their level. Now, we're not telling you to isolate yourself from your friends and family, but do limit your time with people who criticize and make hurtful remarks to you. To make a positive change, you're going to have to find a support group with like-minded ideals and beliefs.

Spend more time with those who add value to your life. Explore all the possibilities by expanding within. When you know the reasons why, you can reach your destiny sooner. But here's a stronger motivator: If you don't change course, you'll be at the same place one, five, and ten years from now; the same income, life, and sense of dissatisfaction.

Your deepest desire is the heart of your purpose. Do not expect your purpose to be fulfilled unless you commit to it wholeheartedly. Don't wake up one day realizing that you've missed out on your life. We all know that some people succeed in life while others suffer one failure after another. What is the difference between successful and unsuccessful individuals? We can tell you the reason in just one word: *focus*. According to quantum physics, the act of focusing actually causes changes in energy fields that automatically produce a physical change in your surroundings. So what exactly is the meaning of the word *focus*? We believe it means:

- Maximum clarity about your goal or desire

- Having a fixed vision with no deviations

- Concentrating your entire attention and energy toward your goal or desire

If you focus on a desire for a long period of time, it lingers in your mind. This creates a feeling. We feel good if we focus on what makes us happy and bad if we focus the other way around. We need to learn how to have the right focus. Focus is a skill that can be employed with our everyday efforts. The ability to focus on various aspects of our goals can generate a large amount of energy to solve problems and move us in the direction of success. When you pay attention to what you're focusing on, you'll see an immediate change in your results. There is no magic pill for success, no secret handbook hidden under a gum tree on top of a mountain; success comes to people who maintain a constant state of focus on their goals. People who are successful and accomplish all they want in life have intently followed the steps to their goals.

Have You Achieved Your Dreams?

What drives you? What do you truly want out of this life? Do you want to be financially independent? Spend more time with your family? Become a famous author and speaker? What are the results you desire for your life, your business, and your family? So, have you achieved your lifelong dream? No? Why not? Take a moment and seriously think about this question. What is keeping you from accomplishing what you want in this life? Could it be your focus?

Your life is a perfect reflection of where you're placing your focus. As you focus more on what you do want and less on what you don't want, you become the conscious creator of your own precious life. Do you need to re-evaluate your life and decide to either change your focus and attitude or give up on your dreams? Please don't misunderstand us; we're not saying you should quit if you aren't at the level of success you want to be. We are saying that if you aren't where you want to be in your personal or professional life, then you need to take a step back from your everyday efforts and gain clarity as to whether you need to start living in a different manner or find a different occupation. It's been said that about 70 per cent of people are in the wrong kind of occupation for their natural skills! No wonder so many people are either unhappy in their work or achieve only modest levels of success. We all have undiscovered talents. We have abilities that we don't appreciate or don't think we have at all.

We often get completely caught up in our day-to-day routines. This prevents us from stepping back from our work, reflecting on our lives and our business, and re-evaluating what we really want to do. It is imperative to your success and your happiness to take the time to reflect. One of the most compelling reasons why we don't get the results we want in life is our lack of focus on what is vital, important, and success-oriented. It is the missing ingredient that can cause well-intentioned people to fall far short of their goals.

The power of focus means that you begin. Too many people never get started. They have the idea, the desire, and the dream, yet they lack the ever-important focus. But what if you do have focus and you're still not getting the results you want in this life? Again, take a moment and evaluate this question thoroughly. Are you truly focused, or do you drift between projects and activities? We live in a society of instant gratification. On-demand movies, the Internet, iTunes – whatever we want is basically at our disposal, so it's only natural for us to become impatient in regards to achieving our goals.

Unfortunately, you can't log on to a website and download your dreams. The universe gives us what we need when we're ready. This is a difficult concept for many to understand, so as a result they lose their focus, their drive, and their consistent movement toward the one result that they have dreamed and planned and worked for. Make a firm commitment and don't give up, no matter how long it takes. True focus is managing your time, making your commitment a priority, and never quitting, no matter how many challenges you encounter. Face your dreams with the idea that the end results far outweigh any obstacle.

You Become What You Focus On

We spend a lot of time thinking, yet how much effort do we consciously put in to managing our thoughts? Have you ever noticed that what you focus on becomes reality? This is true in all aspects of life. Many years ago there was a study done. The researchers wanted to determine if there was a relationship between expectations and focus and eventual outcomes. The result was called the Pygmalion Effect. In essence, the study found that what you consistently believe or focus on will eventually come to pass or become reality in your life. The winter is a great example of the power of focus. As the weather gets colder, more and more people start talking about the flu and sickness. No wonder the doctors' offices are jam-packed – so many people shift their attention to the thought of getting sick. The same is true with money. If you spend your days obsessing over how much money you don't have, you inevitably fall deeper and deeper into debt. Instead, you have to think positively. Consciously block out negative thoughts and stop indulging in activities that distract you. You do have the power to affect your experiences by paying attention to what you focus upon.

It is difficult to have absolute focus on one thing that you are doing without being distracted. Ask even the most focused thinker, and he or she will tell you it is difficult not to be distracted in a given situation. Focus is like a strong magnetic force, in that whatever you focus on comes toward you and you are drawn toward it. As with any magnet, however, the more metal items it is attracting, the weaker the bond. This is the same in life. The example above illustrates the importance of specializing in our lives and having one focus toward which we are aiming.

When you have multiple projects going on and have overcommitted yourself, nothing gets done well. You're simply spread too thin, and you end up feeling scattered. It may seem unrealistic and unimaginable to stop multi-tasking, because you've been doing it for so long. But if you're feeling even slightly overwhelmed, it's not working for you. Our minds allow us to focus on only one thing at a time. We might be reading and watching TV at the same time, but our minds are switching back and forth instead of focusing on both. The more balls we try to juggle with a lack of focus, the more likely we are to miss a catch and end up trying to run in several different directions. When you have just one focus, you become much more productive.

Finding a Support System

It doesn't matter where you came from, how intelligent you are, what talents you have, or how big your dreams are – you will not succeed without active support. This may sound like a discouraging statement, but let us explain further. How many people do you know who are more successful than you? What are these people doing, or what do they know that you don't? If you examine their lives closely, you'll find one common factor they share. They all surround themselves with people who think just like they do. Do you think that Bill Gates or Oprah associate with people who constantly see the negative side of life? No, they spend their valuable time with those who share their visions and goals. The most successful entrepreneurs understand that their success comes in direct relation to how effective they are at building relationships with like-minded people. The bottom line is that there are many people who are willing to help; you just have to let go of your pride and ask.

We knew that we had hit a crisis point when our bank wouldn't extend us any more credit. We didn't have the luxury of time to wait for assistance from the government. We needed the help now. Our banker mentor offered us some valuable advice that no one else did. He told us to go to a real estate agent, cut our losses, and get out. Right then we realised that if we were willing to listen, someone always had a nugget of free advice. We met with an agent, gave the figure we wanted, and told him that he had 30 days to sell it. With unwavering belief and faith, we had an offer on day 30!

My mastermind group was a fabulous tool to help me build up my confidence. The people in this group understood what I was going through and encouraged me with words like "Yes, you can". It was this support that gave me the confidence and self-esteem to say, "I can do anything, and it is all going to be okay, and my life is going to be better than I ever imagined."

– Geraldine

Attaching ourselves to people who were successful, consulting a qualified professional, and finding a mentor pulled us out of our situation. We had no money, yet we were blessed by finding the right people in various roles who were willing to help us. The best aspect of this was that it didn't cost any money. Far too often, people fear they can't get help because they don't have any money. We found just the opposite to be true. Look for mentors in the field you need help with. These could perhaps be retired individuals, or maybe even members of a network marketing group. Looking back at our crash, we should have consulted with these types of people when we were losing money, not after it was gone.

When you want to make a success out of your life, the first action you must take is to find people who are already a success in your chosen endeavour. Once you find them, make it a point to talk to them about what made them successful.

To increase your understanding of the issue you face, valuable information can also be obtained by talking to people who fit the following categories:

- Others who have made money in your desired field

- Those who have lost money in your desired field

- Those who have extensive experience in your field

- Those who just recently started

You will find that everyone has a different story to tell, and a different strategy. There are people who've made several mistakes and persisted through the bad times. Then there are people who made their fortunes by accident. It doesn't matter how they did it; all that truly matters is that they accomplished what you want to accomplish.

All of these people will shorten your learning curve. Not only will they tell you what to do, they will also tell you what *not* to do. Often, learning to avoid mistakes is more important than anything else. As you are talking to these people, you will also see that each individual has a different idea as to what they want to accomplish from their endeavours and how much time, money, and effort they are willing to spend. Some go on to become major successes; others fail miserably.

The best individuals to talk to are people who are working in the area of business that you prefer. If you want to specialize in network marketing, talk to people in that business. Pick their brains and learn all you can from them. These professionals can also become invaluable members of your team as you build your business.

One of the most important people you need to find is a mentor. A mentor will help you learn and understand the ins and outs of all aspects of your venture. Finding a qualified mentor who exactly understands your kind of business will take time, but it is time well spent. It is wise to get recommendations from other professionals, entrepreneurs, and investors, and then make appointments with those recommended. You can look for mentors in your current field or search for specialists. We met with one man who specialised in helping small businesses. We also needed a financial counsellor because we were totally lost. In this case, through our mentor, we were given a clear picture of our circumstances and several options for what needed to be done.

When you meet with your potential mentors, look for people who are eager to communicate their expertise, help you put a game plan in place, keep you on task, and encourage you to succeed. The mentor should be a good fit, and you should feel comfortable accepting his or her help. Again, we stress that the quality of interpersonal communication between you and your mentor cannot be underestimated.

Chapter Questions

1. What are your strengths, and what do you enjoy doing?

2. What values are important to you? Identify your top five.

3. Given that determining your life's purpose is an unfolding process, describe your life's purpose as it is for you right now.

4. As you work through this exercise, does a symbol or slogan come to mind to express the way you would like your life to be?

5. Have you found a mentor or an ally, and have you asked that person to assist you?

Chapter IV

Uncovering the Possibilities: Self-esteem and Self-worthiness

Of all the judgments we pass in life, none is more important than the judgment we pass on ourselves.

– Nathaniel Branden

The way we think about everything in our lives depends on how we feel about ourselves. For us, hitting financial rock bottom damaged our self-esteem. Once you lose your sense of worth, it becomes easy to beat yourself up about any past mistakes. Falling into this pattern is detrimental because it prevents you from moving on and addressing your issues.

Sometimes we experience trials in life. For example, we lost all of our assets, but financial chaos isn't the only tribulation people face. Divorce, death, and even natural disasters, such as the massive bush fires we recently dealt with, can all wreak havoc on our sense of self-esteem. We had to make massive changes in this area in order to regain a positive cash flow. The same is true for everyone else. If you don't feel good about who you are on the inside, you're living a lie on the outside.

If you perceive yourself to be unworthy or inadequate, your self-esteem suffers as well. With low self-esteem, we tend to duck for cover rather than charge ahead full force with a set of solutions.

When you make the decision to change your thought process and rid your mind of any negative images, you are able to let go of the past and move on to a brighter future. Once you develop a strong sense of self, you're more apt to look at life as limitless rather than limited.

Our Greatest Power

How many times have you lain down, hoping for a good's night's sleep, only to toss and turn, cover your ears with the pillow, and eventually turn on the TV to quiet the voices in your head? Now, we're not talking about a Linda-Blair scenario where you levitate and hear things like, "Freddy is the devil." We are referring to the thoughts that bombard us. We've all had sleepless nights due to the constant stream of what-ifs and why-nots. These thoughts also race through our minds just as much during the day. Our thoughts are the single most important factor contributing to our success in life. As a young child, your parents, teachers, coaches, and other influential people passed their thoughts on to you. Sounds strange, we know. Stop and think about this for a minute. Where did each of your thoughts come from?

Thoughts are like the old stories passed down from generation to generation. Remember when you were a kid at camp, and a secret was passed around the picnic table at lunch? The original message of "I think Billy's cute" morphed into "Billy's sister is a mute." Unfortunately, our thoughts change along the way, just as the stories of yesteryear lose their authenticity. To this day, many of us still don't walk under a ladder, and we think twice about opening an umbrella in the house. Now we all know that we won't get mowed down by an ice cream truck the moment we step out from underneath that ladder, and the house isn't going to collapse and disappear into a sinkhole when we open the umbrella, so why do we cringe at the thought of these things? These are fun examples, but sadly, some of our thoughts are damaging and self-sabotaging. Thoughts such as "I'm not good enough" or "I'm not smart enough" have the potential to prevent you from accomplishing your dreams. Now don't slam this book shut and throw it against the wall thinking that your life is over because your parents told you that if you don't work hard you'll never make any money.

So the question is, how do we let go of our negative self-images and move forward in life? Before we can make any attempt to improve our perceptions about ourselves, we first need to understand one vital fact. Our greatest power isn't inside our biceps and triceps, but rather in the tremendous strength of our thoughts. You can lift weights every day, bench press twenty times your weight, and be in the best physical shape of your life, but if you're not healthy mentally, you are vulnerable. You see, most people don't realise the need to strengthen their internal selves. Our thoughts create our lives, and if we want to move forward, we have to control them. To change our results, we first have to change the way we think. There's hope! All of us can change our thoughts.

To rewire your thought process, you first need to know how the mind works. Now don't worry, we're not going to go into a heap of psychological mumbo-jumbo and tell you to call everyone you've ever insulted and apologize. This is just straightforward information to help you get the life you deserve. Before you know it, your negative limiting beliefs will be out the door and replaced with productive and encouraging ones. After all, your mind is the driving force for your life, and without the proper knowledge of how it works, the road to self-discovery would be difficult.

Our minds are a collection of all our experiences. It is like the Smithsonian. Everything from the beginning of time is on display, and you can visit any time you wish. Understanding this process helps you learn to assess your life and ultimately find happiness.

We all think in terms of pictures. When we think of our ideal lives, we don't see a group of graphs and charts detailing how much money we have. Instead, we think of a mansion on the proverbial hill. Actually, we see an international coaching business in which we help others to live the lives of their dreams. We see a vacation home in Belgium to which we can retreat to visit our son. We see a life filled with five-star restaurants and theatre outings.

What about you? What does your ideal life look like? We'd be willing to bet that the life of your dreams doesn't look like a dead-end job and stack of overdue bills. Do us a favour. Stop reading for a moment, mark this page, and then go to your child's room and raid the crayon box. If you don't have any children, rummage through your junk drawer for some old Textas. Now, using the space below, draw a picture of what your ideal life looks like – yes, stick figures will be fine! If you can't draw, then write about it. Go ahead; it will all make sense in time. Remember, you think in pictures. We want you to start seeing the picture of the life you want.

Our thoughts are very influential in that we either use them to create a life of unlimited prosperity and abundance or one of lack and limitation. So many times we hear of people who blame their financial status on circumstances or other people. This would have been very easy for us to do. We could have blamed the economy, or numerous other things, for the failure of our bed and breakfast. But why? How would that have helped us? It wouldn't have. It would have just kept us in the same negative, gloom-and-doom frame of mind. One of the most common excuses we hear in our coaching is, "I could be a millionaire, too, if I had a university degree." Or, "If I would just lose ten kilos I'd feel better about myself and could get that job I've always wanted." It doesn't matter if you have a wall full of diplomas or are the thinnest person at the office; your success in life does not depend on any person, place, or thing: it depends solely on your own ability to master your thoughts.

Understanding Our Minds

Sir John Eccles, an Australian neurologist and Nobel laureate, determined that the human brain is only 10 per cent functional at best. The potential of the human brain is infinite. A simple look at the screen of an MRI machine, or the results of a PET scan, offers incontrovertible evidence that we do not use all of our brains all of the time. Unlike a computer hard drive, our brains have unlimited storage. We have an unlimited capacity to learn.

Earlier we asked you to draw a picture of your ideal life. More than likely, you didn't have any trouble creating that picture. But what if we asked you to draw a picture of your mind? What would that look like? A giant head of cauliflower? Most people mistake the image of our brains with that of our minds. These two are not interchangeable. They are very different entities. The brain is an organ which controls our movement and blood pressure, while the mind is an activity. Our minds think in terms of pictures. For us to have a true understanding of the mind, we must have a clear mental picture as well. Since our thoughts are visual, we need a picture of our minds. Below, you'll find a simplistic but informative drawing which will help bring forth an accurate image of the mind.

Conscious Mind

Ideas form, senses interpreted, choices made, information accepted or rejected

Subconscious Mind

Cannot choose, must accept all information from conscious mind, storehouse of habits and

emotions.

Body

Automatic response to subconscious mind

Action → **Results**

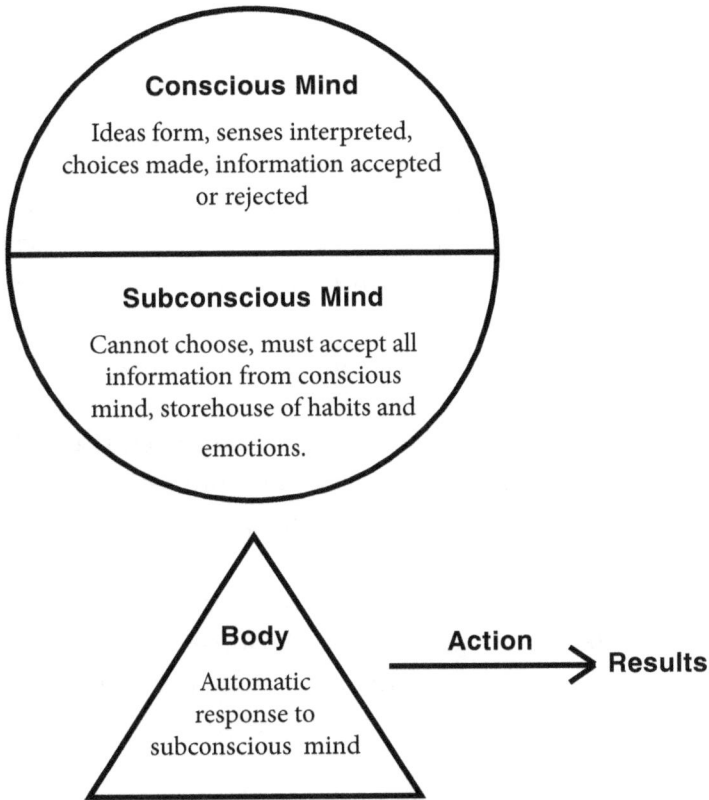

Our minds are separated into two states of consciousness:

- The conscious

- The subconscious

This doesn't mean to imply that we have two minds, but that these various states are coexistent. The two are so important that we're going to discuss them individually.

The Conscious Mind

The conscious part of the mind uses the five senses: sound, taste, touch, smell, and sight. It also thinks logically and has free will to accept or reject any idea. No one but you chooses your thoughts. No person or circumstance can make you choose what you think about. Your ideas or thoughts are your own. So why do the thoughts of our earliest influences become our own? A child's conscious mind is similar to a sponge in that it absorbs everything it touches. As we mentioned earlier, you received a legacy of thoughts from your parents, teachers, clergy, coaches, and any other early mentors. They passed on to you their beliefs and ideas, many of which were meant to help you. Unfortunately, along with all the helpful messages imparted by this process, they also passed on their own fears, false beliefs, and prejudices. This conditioned you to accept many limitations. Because these beliefs were given to us at such an early age by people who loved us or cared for us, it is hard for us to question them and learn to free ourselves from those paradigms that limit us and interfere with our growth.

The Subconscious Mind

This is the motor of the brain. It works all the time. No coffee breaks, lunch hours, or sick leave. It's on the go 24/7. Our subconscious minds are where our habits and belief systems are formed. Since it has no ability to reject any idea or thought, it simply accepts every suggestion made to it. The subconscious is also where our memories are stored. Our self-image consists of memories which have an emotional connection to the past and cannot help us when attempting to break limiting behaviours. The subconscious mind is the sum total of our past experiences and memories. What we feel, think, or do forms the basis of our experience.

Our subconscious minds have no choice but to accept what we think. They have to accept the pictures we give them. Every thought you choose to let into your subconscious mind has to become part of your subconscious mind. Any thought you consciously choose to impress upon the subconscious mind over and over again becomes fixed in this part of your personality. Have you ever had to give a presentation in front of a large audience or give a speech in front of your peers? You're standing just off the stage, waiting to be announced. Just as you hear your name, you have a thought like "I hope I don't trip" or "I hope I don't stutter." These thoughts are not uncommon and occur to even the most seasoned presenters. Did you know the fear of public speaking is greater than the fear of dying?

We all have a tendency to have repetitive negative thoughts, especially regarding events or situations that make us feel vulnerable or uncomfortable. Our thoughts can become so repetitive that they interfere with our ability to function on a daily basis. This causes anxiety, which in turn produces more repetitive thoughts. We can break this vicious cycle through awareness. We have a great deal of control over our thoughts once we are aware of them.

Until your repetitive thoughts cease, your results will continue. These repetitive thoughts take over and infect our minds. Our thoughts are massive and powerful and control our destiny. Our predominant thoughts must be focused on, and be in harmony with, all the good in our lives, not what we don't have or can't do.

The Body

This is the shell for your thoughts and feelings. Go back to the diagram and notice how much larger the mind is than the body. The mind influences every aspect of the body.

The body responds automatically to the subconscious mind. Suppose that, over the years, the conditioning of your subconscious mind has been toward anger. If an event occurs which is uncomfortable for you, the subconscious mind will link that feeling with its programmed condition and instantly you will feel angry. If your past programming in relation to money has been one of lack and never having enough, then the mere arrival of a bill in the mail will automatically arouse feelings of worry and anxiety and you will very likely respond by complaining or blaming others for your situation.

The Intellectual Faculties

We are all born with five senses: sight, taste, touch, hearing, and smell. By the age of five, most children have a complete understanding of their ability to use their five senses to understand the world and the environment around them. The five senses are limited to telling us and showing us what already "is". They have no power to create or transform.

Intellectual skills do have the power to create and transform your habits. They are present in each one of us, and each identifies a powerful area of thought that we can use to change our habits and transform our lives.

The six intellectual skills are:

1. Will

2. Imagination

3. Perception

4. Reasoning (both deductive and inductive)

5. Intuition

6. Memory

These skills are always at work. In order for us to utilize our minds, we must exercise these skills, which are much like mental muscles. Your ability to have the life of your dreams starts with your decisions. The ability to make sound decisions is directly related to the development, integration, and strength of these six faculties which, when exercised, expand infinitely. Let's take a closer look at each one of these.

Will

Will enables us to hold an image, idea, or thought that we want in our conscious minds until it embeds itself into our subconscious. This allows it to manifest itself in our lives. The will allows us to take any subconscious idea that may have been present in our minds since childhood and change it. We do this by intense concentration over time and with repetition. Any habit that we want to stop or change encounters our will. The term "will power" has been used in conjunction with weight loss, addiction, and exercise, but it can also be used to stop habitual thoughts or self-doubt.

Imagination

This is our creative power. Great minds have created and invented numerous things, ranging from artificial hearts to the Internet, against all doubt and odds. They used the power of imagination combined with the other intellectual skills. Your imagination is either imagining how you can do something or why you can't.

Perception

This creates meaning from events or experiences in our lives. We interpret these based on past events and programming. In terms of perception, everything is relative. Nothing has meaning, or is good or bad, until we think it so. Consequently, each person will have a different perception or interpretation of exactly the same event or object.

Never underestimate the role of perception in our daily lives. It has the power to alter our attitudes and the courses of our lives almost without our notice. It takes much strength of will to change perceptions we have held for a long time.

Reasoning

Reasoning is our ability to understand the events in our world. Deductive reasoning is our default thought process that insures that we will continue to be a product of our environment. Deductive reasoning relies for guidance on your current understanding and conditioning at the subconscious level.

When you are reasoning deductively, you will quickly reject anything that doesn't match your current understanding or paradigms. This guarantees that you will continue to act on ideas that keep that paradigm in place, and you are likely to reject an idea that would move your life or wealth forward. You will also likely stay in your comfort zone when you are being deductive, and your attitudes will be created by your surrounding environment, rather than creating the environment that surrounds you. You are purely deductive when your environment creates you, and you are being inductive when you create your own environment. Inductive reasoning (true thinking) occurs when you use your intuition, perception, will, imagination, and memory to analyze new ideas, and then create and support the picture of what you want to see manifest with new thought patterns.

Intuition

Often referred to as our "sixth sense", intuition is our ability to connect with another individual without even knowing or speaking to them. When we meet someone who immediately makes us feel good or positive, that person projects a positive energy, and our intuition senses it. When we meet someone who makes us feel negative or scared, our intuition immediately warns us of the negativity. Developing your intuition to tune in to the highest level of those around you allows you to see through all the noise of conversation and immediately understand the essence of those around you.

Memory

This is our ability to recall previous events and experiences. Many of us tend to remember only our failures, and those memories seem to linger and be more intense than our memories of success. It is important to use our memories to bolster our confidence and self-esteem as we try something new. At one point, everything was new to us – yet we learned. We must exercise our memories to work in our favour and remind us that we can do anything we set our minds to. Consciously focusing on past success, no matter how small, improves our overall self-confidence. Every person reading this book has succeeded at multiple things in life to get to this point. Claim those successes, and remember them every time you set your course for a new journey in life.

How Does Your Body Reflect Your Attitude?

Have you ever stood in front of a mirror and asked yourself, "What is my body saying about me?" This is a difficult question for most people to answer. Do you have slouched shoulders, no make-up, and wrinkled clothes? One of our favourite authors, Tony Robbins, believes that by changing your physiology you can most definitely change your results. The best example of this is someone who has lost a large amount of weight. We've all seen this happen, whether it was to ourselves or a spouse, family member, or friend. Levels of confidence and self-esteem skyrocket. People are no longer content to sit on the sidelines of life; they want to experience all they've been missing. Sadly, the opposite is true for anyone who has experienced a financial crash.

I remember my own physiology as we went through our financial crash. Geraldine was constantly telling me to stand up straight, put my shoulders back, and hold my head up. She became so frustrated with me at times because she made many attempts to have a meaningful conversation with me, yet I sat listless and wouldn't say a word. I knew how miserable I was, but thought I could keep it on the inside and no one would know. How wrong I was. My emotional state was written all over me. I remember looking at myself in the mirror one morning and thinking, Who is this old man staring back at me?

– Bill

How many of you can relate to this? You have a closet full of beautiful clothes, yet you wear the same pair of shorts and T-shirts each day. Even during the worst of circumstances, it is imperative to regain a positive image of yourself, and this can't be done by wearing scruffy clothes and sitting apart from everyone else in the room. Think about the types of people you'll attract in that state of mind. It won't be the positive ones who are willing to succeed at all costs. Once you allow yourself to fall backward, you're basically repelling those who can benefit you the most. We speak from experience.

I spent several months crying and asking why this happened to me. I told myself that I was a good person who helped others, so why and how could something like this happen to me? The occasional time without make-up quickly became an everyday event. I was wallowing in so much self misery that I didn't even want to fix my hair, put on lipstick, or leave the house. It wasn't until I started my mentor program with Bob Proctor that I began to realise what a mistake I had been making. On one of the first calls with Bob, we were asked to rate our clothes, hair, and physical appearance. I'll never forget standing in front of that mirror thinking, My goodness, I've really let myself go. I ate through my crisis and had gained weight as some sort of protective cushion so I could never feel so bad again. I made the change that night and started wearing make-up, dressing better, and monitoring my diet.

– Geraldine

We realised that we ate not because our bodies needed food; rather, our minds were hungry for answers. And until we were able to take an open, honest look at ourselves, we fed our mouths instead of our minds. Many of the answers were we searching for were found with the help of a life coach.

Changing your diet to include the correct amount of vitamins, minerals, and nutrients is also essential to maintaining a well-balanced life; our bodies need the right nutrition to work at their best. One of the most important reasons to alter your diet is to achieve and maintain a healthy body weight. People who are overweight are at increased health risk for diseases including heart disease, diabetes, stroke, osteoarthritis, gallbladder disease, gout, and certain types of cancer. Losing as little as 5 to 10 per cent of your body weight will improve your health and overall well-being. Reducing the amount of stress in our lives is also important to our overall health. Stress lowers our immune systems and often leads to depression. There are a wide variety of stress-reduction techniques, from simple meditation and breathing exercises to yoga, which is a full system for relaxation and de-stressing. All will keep you balanced and full of energy.

Relationships

Evaluating your relationships during a time of strife is beneficial in that it will help you to see the true friends who are willing to stand by you and be genuinely happy for your future success. Often, we believe we have to hold on to people in our lives because they're family, or because we've known them for 20 years. Lives change, and people grow in different directions. When we started our transformation, some people close to us had a difficult time with our decisions. But we knew deep in our souls that this was our purpose in life. So the question you'll have to ask yourself, just like we did, is: Does this person support you, or constantly bring you down? This is a tough question that we've had to answer many times, but if you're truly following your purpose in life, you will connect with other encouraging, likeminded people. As an individual, you will feel more alive and challenged as you pursue your own endeavours. You will learn much you can share with your family. You will grow as an individual as you make it a priority to strike a balance in your relationships.

Chapter Questions

1. Complete a self-esteem analysis. What is your self-talk? What do you say to yourself about yourself?

2. Physiology – what does your body language and posture tell you about you?

3. Appearance – rate yourself and comment on grooming and dress.

4. Using the ideas from this chapter, list six things you will undertake as a commitment to improve your self-esteem.

Chapter V

An Inspired Vision of the Future: Dreaming

Empty pockets never held anyone back. Only empty heads and empty hearts can do that.

– Norman Vincent Peale

Stop for a moment and think about a fingerprint. There are no two alike. Even identical twins have different ones. Granted, the twins may be mirror images of one another, but different just the same. Each fingerprint is unique and specific to only one person in the world. In Chapter III, we discussed finding our purpose in life. Sadly, most people settle for pursuing a career that satisfies their basic human wants and needs, but they never really think beyond that to what their lives could be about. Like fingerprints, we each have a designated reason for being placed on this earth. So if you truly want success in life, and by this we're not just referring to money, you must find out what you're meant to do in life.

Why is it that so many don't live according to this principle? It's simple. We make every attempt to live according to what society deems acceptable, and we stop pursing what we truly want. In our coaching business, we talk about finding your "B" in life. What this entails is looking to see what you aspire to in life, and then learning where you are in relation to this, which we call your "A".

We went through life with some vague idea of what our "A" was, and we focused on that until we learned to dream and follow our purpose. Now we take steps every day toward our "B" through our dreams.

When we decided to embark on our new life, some people couldn't handle the choice we made. Many times we heard (and still hear) statements like, "Why are you two doing this? You should be preparing for retirement, not starting over!" Ironically, our financial crash enabled us to look at our lives with openness and genuine honesty. When we met with our mentors, they asked us what it was that we really wanted to do. Out of this difficult question, we learned to stop worrying about what everyone else thinks and, more importantly, learn how to dream again.

If you have children or spend any amount of time around them, you know firsthand the wonderment of dreams. Whilst we, as adults, view the world through logic and reason, these little ones look at their surroundings with wide-eyed imagination. But dreaming is discouraged. Why is this? Did you ever sit in a classroom and stare out the window and dream of walking on Mars or flying above the clouds? Stop and think about your childhood for a minute. How many times do you remember your parents or teachers telling you to "stop daydreaming" or to "be realistic"? Some other putdowns to dreaming include:

- Dreaming isn't realistic.

- I don't remember how to dream.

- Dreaming is for kids, not adults with responsibilities.

- Dreamers are people who don't accomplish their goals.

Gradually, many have come to believe that all of these misconceptions about dreams are true. Why is it that as we mature, we lose the sense that anything is possible? One reason is that we're conditioned to do so as we grow. In the baby boomer generation, young girls didn't have the option of a dream career. They basically had three choices: teacher, nurse, or secretary.

In my family, we didn't have a choice about our future. We were to go to university and work in a professional environment. As a little girl, I took piano lessons and sang. I loved every minute of it, but I never once thought that I could do it for a living. It wasn't an option for me. So I did what I thought would please both my parents and myself. I studied to become a music teacher. Now that I have let myself dream again, I've written many songs and published my own albums.

– Geraldine

From our earliest awareness, our parents and other influential people in our lives discouraged us from dreaming. Have you ever been told to stop letting your imagination run wild? Or that you're just imagining things? This statement is so close to the absolute truth. What you create – all the circumstances of your life – is being imagined. There is nothing else that we could be doing. All that we seek to be or have will first be developed in our dreams.

How different would our world be now if the past generations were encouraged to dream? Who wants to live in a world of limits? Not us. We want to live in a world where we can put on a rocket jet pack and fly to work, or step into a machine and travel though time. What about the Internet? A little more than a decade ago, no one thought such a thing was possible.

A dream is a state of mind where all things are experienced as real. Dreams are powerful and are an intermediary step between thought and world. Thoughts are experienced in our minds before they are manifested into physical reality. As important as this step is in the process of creating, it is the least explored on a conscious level. It is the easiest step to move into from our conscious state and can be accessed at will. Just close your eyes and start dreaming.

Our dreams give us a safety zone, which we enter for all kinds of reasons; it's practical and recreational. It is a tool that works on demand and has unlimited resources. It's a perfect testing ground where problems can be worked out and we can create anything that we can imagine. We build models in our dreams in preparation for their creation in the physical realm. All of our thoughts can be explored and examined. Working through our dreams is the best way to experience having or doing something before it is made manifest. This was the case with our coaching business, Teggelove Mentoring and Coaching.

Living without Limits

Everything in life is made twice, first in our minds and then in reality. Through dreams, you can experience a new life without the restriction of old belief systems, guilt, morality, punishment, condemnation, justification, or anything else. It's your safe haven where no one can enter. It is truly the only place that you can be alone with your thoughts. You are free from physical bonds or limitations. You can fly for as long and as high as you want. You can crash, burn, barnstorm, or land safely, without fear.

Moving into the realm of your dreams is not to be feared, but anticipated with awe and wild abandon. Fear not the power you possess. Develop your imagination, exercise it, and use it effectively to manifest the physical items that you desire in your life. Dream the life that you really want, and begin to live it. One of our favourite books, *The Secret,* tells us to focus on the positive dreams, not the nightmares. We can change the future through the use of our dreams. By persistently imagining what you really want, you can discard the old script and introduce a completely new story. In other words, you can free yourself of the handicaps that are holding you back.

The act of dreaming is a wonderful ability of your consciousness. Even with open eyes, you can dream. You can imagine lying on the sand at the beach and feeling the warmth of the afternoon sun. You can even imagine that you are sitting on a mountaintop with the wind blowing through your hair. You can imagine touching icy cold water and letting it flow through your hands.

You can imagine objects that do not exist, and you can imagine that these objects do whatever you decide. They don't have to follow any physical rules. Many inventors have used the power of dreams to think up ideas for new products, machines, and improvements. For example, Albert Einstein's creative thinking epitomises most people's idea of genius. He used his famous thought experiments to justify many of his research findings. His theory of relativity began as a daydream about a man in an elevator. These thought experiments were nothing more than Einstein allowing himself to daydream.

This primary creative mindset is that of possibility thinking. Basically, this means giving yourself permission to dream and think of extraordinary things. Part of giving yourself permission to think in exceptional and creative ways is also giving yourself the opportunity to do so. Too many of us relegate the work of thinking to odd moments in the shower, driving to work, or relaxing on the couch. Think about Thomas Edison, for instance. Where would the world be without his zany idea of a light bulb? The most interesting part is that these imaginings, once you have made them, become part of your memory! It's like a virtual world that does not follow any rules that currently exist.

Your past experience cannot hold you captive as long as you can imagine something better. Most people never engage their imaginations because they don't believe that anything better exists. Can you believe that something better exists for you? This means that once you know you are capable of doing better than you have done up to this point, a new world of opportunity opens up to you. Things cannot go back to the way they have been. Once you have tasted abundance and prosperity, there is no turning back.

You will see possibilities everywhere. It is like walking into a completely dark room and suddenly someone turns on the lights – it takes a minute for you to adjust to the brightness, but once you regain your balance, you move forward purposefully. You are here to create abundance. Abundance is your natural state – your destiny is to live an abundant life. The way to fulfil your destiny is to use your creative imagination to construct the life of your dreams. Once you are clear about what you want, the universe rearranges itself to give you your heart's desire. The Law of Attraction causes what you focus on to be brought into your life. As you focus on abundance, more abundance is brought to you. To develop your imagination, ask the following questions:

- What if…

- How about…

- Why don't we…

Believing Is Seeing

Everything starts in the mind. It is imperative that you understand this. Imagination or visualization is the picturing power of your mind. Your subconscious responds to pictures and images held on your mental screen. It may be said that your subconscious is the contractor which will build your life. You are the architect; your imagination is the blueprint. You are constantly running a mental movie with yourself as star of the show. These images determine your personal behaviour and the kind of life you lead. You have the power to mentally create a new life for yourself. Whatever you visualize, you can have. All you must do is see yourself as having achieved your desire. Once you do this, consider your wish accomplished. For you are a self-fulfilling prophecy. What you are thinking about today is a clear indication of what you will be experiencing in the future.

In the movie *Field of Dreams*, Kevin Costner kept hearing the same voice repeatedly whisper, "If you build it, he will come." The same is true with imagination. If you can imagine it, it can be created. Let's assume you want to earn an extra $10,000 in the next few months. Start using your imagination:

- Visualize holding $10,000 in your hands.

- Imagine how it feels against you palms.

- Imagine how you'll feel when you buy all those items you've dreamed of owning.

- Imagine how they'll look in your house. Or how you'll look wearing the new wardrobe you purchased.

By activating this process, you are already training your mind for the event of claiming $10,000. Your mind will start bringing up other pictures and stories when you do this exercise. The uncertainties of the mind will vanish when you consistently rely on your imagination to bring you what you want in life. Do it often, until you see exactly what you desire as actually happening, and no other thoughts, feelings, or pictures surface that are not aligned with your goal.

What this means to us is that you can use your mental images to create what your future can become. Challenge yourself to make your life match your vision. It does not matter what your current situation or circumstance is – you can use visualisation to transcend any situation that does not match your imagined destiny. Our son, Michael, utilised visualisation. Once he harnessed this power, his world opened up for him. While he was training for the National Road Championship in cycling, we took him to a sports psychologist who taught him to visualise his perfect race. After working with her, Michael put his visualisations on a CD, and he listened to it every night for 12 months before the race. The race unfolded exactly as he had visualized. He not only won the race, but taught us the importance of this technique as well. We went home from the race with the realisation that visualisation is real.

The power of visualisation is one of the greatest forces in the universe, but you must act upon your visions. There are four essential steps for becoming successful:

- Purpose

- Dream

- Plan

- Action

Creative visualization takes us a step further than just forming mental images. It causes our dreams to come into existence. It creates or originates; it produces and brings about. When we are creatively visualising something, we are actually causing it to come into being because it has been formed, for the first time, in our minds. Our images contain creative power. They are changed through the power of creative intelligence. The actual means by which things come into being in the outer world is a mystery. Yet we know that if we plant an acorn in the ground, it will produce a massive oak tree. We do not know nature's secret for drawing the substance from the soil to make this new creation. The image or picture of the tree is hidden within the acorn. An idea is like the seed you plant when you want a certain crop. It produces whatever you plant: squash, tomatoes, flowers, trees, or shrubs. Everything depends upon the nature of the seed. Whatever idea you hold in your imagination, whether it is negative or positive, constructive or destructive, it will bring forth its own kind. Like attracts like.

Visualisation can be used to overcome financial, health, and relationship problems, or any other type of problem you may have. We must never think of any situation as hopeless or irresolvable. The belief that we are on the path to self-destruction is simply not true. There have been prophets of doom and gloom since the beginning of recorded history, but they have been wrong every time. All problems are really opportunities in disguise. Bearing this in mind, it behoves us to carefully examine every so-called crisis in our lives for the hidden opportunity in it. The conscious phase of mind power is the most limiting because it is dependent on the outside world. Its information comes through the five senses. Since our senses often deceive us, we frequently accept false concepts, values, and beliefs. By effectively using visualisations, you can create solutions to any problem. You can take a successful idea and mould and modify it to work in an even better way, or you can start from scratch and invent something new and outrageous – the sky's the limit!

But if this is all possible, then why aren't we busy doing it? Why aren't we using our visualisations creatively? Well, the truth is we're always using them for one item or another. The problem is that most people seldom focus their visualisations in the direction of their real desires. If you're thinking about (visualising) what you want half the time, and half the time you're thinking about what you don't want, what do you think you will end up with? Probably a big zero, don't you imagine? Wouldn't the two opposing visualisations just cancel each other out?

But what if you were to spend 75 per cent of your time joyfully envisioning what you want? That would only leave 25 per cent for worry, anger, fear, or doubt. How would your results improve? And as you practice and learn to accentuate the positive and eliminate the negative, visualise how you could vastly improve your odds – maybe even up to 100 per cent. Then you could start creating your life exactly the way you want it.

The conscious mind is objective. It observes and is rational. It is where our willpower comes from and may be likened to a guard at the door. Protecting the access route to the subconscious mind, the conscious mind screens all incoming data and allows the subconscious to accept only that which it perceives as the truth, no matter how faulty.

What we see with our conscious minds often deceives us. We look at the horizon, and the sky and earth seem to meet; a rainbow seems to disappear into the ground; railroad tracks seem to come together in the distance. These distortions are the result of false images and messages from our conscious minds. Relating this concept to the human predicament, sickness, poverty, worry, despair, and hopelessness are faulty images we have accepted from our conscious minds and chosen to perpetuate in our subconscious minds.

To free ourselves from the limitations of our conscious minds, we must turn within, for here is the source of truth. It is not in the outside world. To continue to look for it externally is to continue to experience those conditions which have been holding us back. For this reason, we must listen to our subconscious minds, take that information into our conscious minds and, to create positive and constructive experiences, deliberately program it in our subconscious minds. To do this, we need to take a better look at how we view our lives and the events surrounding us.

Throughout the centuries, successful people have either intuitively or consciously become aware that they possessed a power that would serve them. They called on this power to help them create great works of art, compose, invent, write, and build businesses. Using *heart* as a synonym for *subconscious*, what they were really saying was, "As you think in your subconscious mind, so are you." Although superbly talented and possessing unlimited ability, your subconscious is a servant and, as a servant, must be commanded. It can't motivate itself. In fact, it is an automatic, impersonal mechanism which will faithfully bring about whatever you most persistently impress upon it. It is a valued, competent, trustworthy partner which will supply you with all the necessary information you need to function in a positive, creative manner.

Remember, we said that your subconscious responds according to the beliefs and convictions you hold in your conscious mind. Your conscious mind chooses what it believes to be true and your subconscious accepts, without question, whatever it dictates. Your subconscious will, therefore, accept failure as readily as success and is, indeed, the means by which you will bring about either.

At this very moment, your subconscious is working for or against you. Through your conscious mind, it senses and records all your physical, intellectual, mental, and emotional experiences and stores the information for further use. The sum total of these experiences determines your present level of awareness.

As we have said, our conscious minds are greatly influenced by our five senses, so it is easy to see why we get confused when we use the conscious mind alone to bring about the right answers to our problems. The five senses often do not report the truth to us, so we accept, reject, and relate everything based on what may be a mistaken certainty. To look at a situation and evaluate the information based on the conscious mind alone is to look at the effect instead of the cause. This makes us value-judge both ourselves and others. We evaluate what we see, hear, and feel as if it were, indeed, the truth. The lives of so many people are plagued with one problem after another because they take actions and make decisions based on faulty awareness.

What we need to do is to train ourselves to look within and visualise the lives we truly desire. As long as we rely on the conscious mind alone, we shall continue to make mistakes and become disappointed and frustrated. The correct thinking process goes like this:

- Use visualisations to give you the guidance you need.

- Use the conscious mind to program this information into the subconscious.

- Command the subconscious to carry out this information.

There is a tremendous power in words. Words can build or destroy your life. They made you what you are right now. Talk is verbalised thinking, and you utter about 20,000 words a day. The way you talk to yourself has a profound effect upon your feelings, actions, and accomplishments. What you say determines practically everything you do. For instance, words can even change your blood pressure, heart rate, and breathing.

The subconscious accepts without question the words we use to program it, whether they are positive or negative. Positive statements or affirmations build your life, while negative statements or affirmations destroy it. The subconscious is then required to carry out these negative commands and so we experience sickness, lack, limitation, and failure.

What you must do is police your speech and turn such self-defeating statements around. The way to program your mind is to use positive affirmations and repeat them over and over again until your subconscious accepts them as reality. In psychology, this is called the Law of Predominant Mental Impression. When you keep saying that you are sick, your subconscious is required to make you sick; if you affirm health, it is required to make you healthy. Never rehearse a contrary situation by saying to yourself that you feel great, then, when someone asks how you are, replying that you feel terrible just to get some sympathy. Switching back and forth only confuses the subconscious, and this will have repercussions in your life.

Now that we've discussed the importance of visualization, we'd like to take the opportunity to demonstrate a technique to strengthen and reinforce your visualisations. Remember, emotion is the carrier of visualisation; no creative act is performed without it. The subconscious responds greatly to feeling and emotion. In our experience, vision boards are one of the best activities to embed positive thoughts into your subconscious mind. As a matter of fact, we believe they are a vital ingredient for finding and following your life's purpose and manifesting your dreams.

Vision boards are simple and relatively easy to complete. After reading the earlier chapters, you now, more than likely, have an idea of how you want your life to be. The next step is to search through magazines, the Internet, and any other source of pictures to find the ones that most represent the life you desire. It is very important to use the exact image of what you want to attract, as whatever you have on your vision board will become part of your reality! After you find the images, apply them along with positive words or statements to a piece of poster board or paper.

Before we go any further, it is important to point out that your vision board is to be lived, not just read. Review it every day and allow the images and words to saturate your subconscious mind. Use it to create a mental map of what you want in life, and make it a part of your daily routine. See the details – colours, places and people – as vividly as you can. Hold the pictures and words clearly in your mind. Most importantly, you must put yourself in the picture.

We chose to place our vision board in a location where we could see it many times a day. Your vision board should be a constant reminder of your vision in life. It will open your mind to creative thinking. The Law of Attraction is closely related to a vision board. Like attracts like, so it makes sense that bombarding yourself with positive images and words daily will change your thought process so that you'll attract what you want in life. Each time you look at your vision board, you're attracting its contents into your life. It is one of the most powerful ways to make the Law of Attraction work for you. Soon you will master the technique of visualisation; in the process, desire will become reality. Live your purpose. Dream big. Visualise yourself having, doing, or being the things you want, and take action. Once you have a vision board and know how to use it effectively, you have the power to succeed at anything.

Chapter Questions

1. Briefly describe your current situation in each of the following areas: family and relationships, finances, physical health, emotional health, and spiritual (not religion, but the longing deep within us) health.

2. As a starting point, what would you like to change in each of these areas?

3. Dream big! List five things you would like to see happen in each area.

4. Of the list you have made, find pictures of three things and display them in a prominent place such as on the fridge or the bathroom mirror.

Chapter VI

Reaching for the Sky: Goals

Goals allow you to control the direction of change in your favor.

– Brian Tracy

Many of you may have heard of the famous Harvard Business School study of goals in which only 3 per cent of the graduating class had specific, written goals for their futures. Twenty years later, that 3 per cent was found to be earning an astounding ten times that of the group that had no clear goals. This story was so fascinating to us, we wanted to include it our book. While conducting the needed research, we found an article in *Fast Company* magazine revealing that no such study had ever been done!

We couldn't believe it. How could this study not exist? Goals are such an important part of life. Business and life coaches, athletes, motivational speakers, and so many other successful people emphasise the importance of not only having goals, but writing them down as well. So the widespread mention of this non-existent study, as well as the need to satisfy our curiosity, fuelled our desire to delve further into the idea of how goal achievement is influenced by writing goals, committing to goal-directed actions, and being accountable for those actions. We discovered that there actually was a study done to prove what we've known to be true for so many years. There is a study demonstrating that writing one's goal enhances goal achievement. However, it was not done at Harvard or Yale, but at Dominican University.

A total of 267 participants were recruited from businesses, organizations, and business networking groups. However, only 149 participants completed the study. The final participants ranged in age from 23 to 72, with 37 males and 112 females. Participants came from the United States, Belgium, England, India, Australia, and Japan and included a variety of entrepreneurs, educators, healthcare professionals, artists, attorneys, bankers, marketers, human services providers, managers, vice presidents, and directors of non-profit organizations. The success of the people in the group who set goals and wrote them down was significantly higher than those in the group who didn't. This study provides empirical evidence for the effectiveness of three coaching tools:

- Accountability

- Commitment

- Writing down your goals

Throughout my life, I've written down my goals and tucked these lists away in one spot or another. Over the past several months, I've been fortunate enough to find some of these lists. I've been able to see my accomplishments and actually place ticks next to the goals I've achieved.

– Bill

To us, goal setting is the crux of coaching; without this process, success can be elusive. With all the discussion about the importance of goals, why is it that so many people don't set them? Brian Tracy's book *Goals* identifies four specific reasons. In our coaching practice, we've confirmed that our clients fall into one or more of these categories.

- Goals are unimportant to some people. With all of the negativity in society today, many resign themselves to the fact that life won't or can't get better. They waste their energies focusing on the negative. Why not eliminate this type of worst-case thinking? Challenge yourself to be the best you can be by setting some goals for a better life.

- Others lack knowledge. We have worked with a number of couples who told us they didn't know how to go about setting goals. The process seemed so overwhelming to them that they did nothing.

- People fear failure. We don't like failure. This is a part of our conditioning. We were taught that failure is a terrible consequence. It's so bad, in fact, we'll do anything, including inaction, to avoid it. But failure is good; you simply have to decide whether you want to fail forward or fail backward. In other words, either you can fail, learn, and move on… or you can fail, get stuck, and give up. The choice is yours. When you're willing to work and take daily action despite any setbacks, you can fail forward and accomplish your goal sooner. Many successful people fail their way to success. Think of Thomas Edison. How many attempts did it take to invent the light bulb? Would you call those failures? Not us; we call them ways not to invent a light bulb.

- People fear rejection. This ties in with failure and is very personal to most of us. If we set goals, talk about them, and write them down for others to see, what happens if we don't accomplish them? We're afraid people will criticize us. To us, however, this as an opportunity to prove ourselves.

Embrace the Unknown

A mistake many people make is to set goals based on what they know they are capable of. There is no inspiration in goals you know how to achieve. In order to stretch and grow, you must have a goal that excites you and scares you, too. You must be inspired to stretch and find new ways of reaching the goal. You must use your ability to dream when deciding on your goals. In order to achieve this, you must start with what you really desire in life. Your dreams are an important part of your growth. They are like a flame burning inside you, fuelling you with the energy to pursue your goal. You feed this flame with your vision of your dream. If your goal doesn't scare you, it's not big enough. If you feel uncomfortable, you are on the right track. In order to grow, you must be outside your comfort zone. Nothing grows inside a comfort zone. When you move outside yours, it will be a bit uncomfortable – and that's a good sign. Get excited by it; celebrate it – you're moving closer to your goal.

How many times have you started a new project, reached for a new goal, or set out to accomplish something incredible, only to abandon the project or goal soon after starting? Maybe it was a savings plan that you only put money into once or twice. Or worse, maybe you used a credit card with the best of intentions to pay it off in three months, only now it is two years later and the interest is more than your original purchase. Why do people often start out with grand aspirations and then quit before even making it halfway through? In a word: *fear*. In fact, fear of "hitting the wall" is the number one reason why people don't achieve their goals. Everyone has a comfort zone, a mental place where they feel at ease. The problem is that if you stay in your comfort zone too long, you don't grow and achieve your goals. All growth takes place outside this zone. But when most people step out, they feel pulled back in by their old habits and ways of thinking. That's when they hit the wall and become frightened. They procrastinate, make excuses, and do any number of things to validate why they should give up and go back to the way things were.

When Geraldine and I started to reduce our debt and accumulate savings, we were breaking new ground. We had never had savings before. We lived off our credit cards and had the mindset of spend now and save later. I thought to myself, I couldn't save money then, how can I save money now, with no income at all? We looked at our finances and realised that in order to pull ourselves back into the black, we needed to set goals. So we broke our larger goals into smaller ones and even set a goal in terms of saving money. As we accomplished this goal, saving money and paying off our debt gradually became easier and less daunting.

– Bill

If you want to stretch yourself, set high goals, or learn new skills, you must step up and embrace the unknown. Use the following strategies to overcome the fear barrier you will face so you can push through to your ultimate objectives.

Make Your Goals Emotional

Logical goals don't normally get you excited. Decreasing your credit card debt by 10 per cent is good, but how would that feel in comparison to paying them off and cutting them up? We're willing to bet that you're a little more than just excited. You're probably ecstatic! When we aren't excited about a goal, we're not willing to do whatever it takes to accomplish it. The key to creating emotional goals is to start with visualization. Create a picture in your mind of achieving your end result. For example, if you want to increase your nest egg, envision yourself looking at your bank statement with a balance of $100,000. Feel the pride of having enough discipline and dedication to set that much money aside. That's an emotional goal.

Next, write down the goal and put a date on when you would like to achieve it. If you miss the date, it doesn't matter; just review and reset. It is no good writing down a goal without establishing a date by which time you will have accomplished it. Don't crowd your goal out by including too many individual action steps. This can actually prevent you from achieving your goals. It is not necessary to know exactly what to do and how to do it before you can start toward your goal. By doing too much preplanning, you'll end up feeling overwhelmed and too scared to even start. So just decide on the goal and map it out along the way. Rather than create action steps, write down ten reasons why you want the goal. Why will it be worth it? You will need this list later when the going gets tough.

Take Notice of When the Fear Appears in Your Life

When you are doing something new, how do you veer off course?

Do you feel fear? Do you procrastinate? Do you worry? Do you make excuses? Do you get distracted easily? For example, if your goal is to pay the bills every Sunday night, you may continually say, "I'll skip tonight and set aside some time tomorrow" (procrastination). Or if your goal is to meet prospective clients, you may get sidetracked from making prospecting calls because your office is messy and you need to clean it first (distraction).

These little annoying instances are nothing more than vain attempts to keep you in your comfort zone. But understanding this process and how it manifests in your life is a fantastic source of energy. Now you know why you are procrastinating, why you're not sleeping well at night, or why you feel fear. You know that it's simply an indication that you're growing. Now you can recognize the sign and can acknowledge that you need to get over the wall. This helps take the pain out of it, so you can continue to move forward. Remember that the world is constantly changing. If you're not moving forward, then you're falling behind.

Take Action toward Your New Goal

Unfortunately, many people feel that they are successful only when they reach the end goal. This isn't the case, for every step you take in the direction of your goal is a success in its own right. Map out your next steps as you go. The key is to simply move in the right direction – you don't have to get there all at once. Yes, you'll have some bumps along the way and make some mistakes, but those are important parts of learning. Your failures are necessary in order for you to get the knowledge you need to push through.

Celebrate When You Hit the Wall

Hitting a wall of fear simply means you are growing. Be happy that you are widening your comfort zone and moving toward your goals. Think of it as building a new house. Before you can get the dream home you've always wanted, complete with granite countertops, custom cabinets, and top-of-the-line appliances, you first need to break through the soil to pour a foundation. You can stand on the edge of the concrete and think to yourself, "This is too much work. How can my new house come from nothing?" Or persist with the project, visualize your home, and watch it manifest from concrete, mortar, and boards to your reality dream home. The same holds true for any worthwhile goal you want to accomplish.

Repetition Is the Key

Keep on and push through! Just like professional athletes who practice and train regularly, the more you persevere and keep moving in the direction of your goal, the better results you'll achieve. When the going gets exceptionally rough, refer to your initial list of ten reasons why you want the goal. Read the reasons you outlined slowly, so you can think about them and envision them. Connect to the emotions of achieving the goal so you stay motivated.

If you don't feel some fear on a regular basis, then realise you're not growing and need to take some serious action... right now. Celebrate the fear factor, be grateful for the opportunities available to you, and always have new goals in mind that you can strive for. As humans, our natural tendency is to grow and to want more out of life. Embrace that mindset as you press on. When you acknowledge the fear barrier in your life and use it to your benefit, you'll have the ability to achieve any goal you set for yourself and reach even greater levels of success.

See the End at the Beginning

To be successful, you must first see the ultimate goal you want to achieve. So instead of starting with "meet more prospects" or "work 80 hours per week", start with your ultimate result. For example, what do you want for your year-end numbers? How much do you want to earn? How many new clients do you want to attract? Whatever you want, make it clear and write it down. Only 3 per cent of people ever write down their goals. And in any company, approximately 3 per cent of the employees rise to top-performer status. Think there's a correlation?

As you design your end result, be sure you choose goals you're passionate about. Remember that people are not moved by rational things; they're moved by emotional things. So while you may want to increase your closing ratio by 30 per cent, that's not a moving image. Instead, see yourself standing in front of your peers at your company's yearly meeting and receiving the Salesperson of the Year award. That's an image that triggers emotion. Whatever you do, don't fall into the trap of just working with no goal in mind. That's the quickest path to frustration and poor results.

Now that you are clear on what you want, do an assessment of where you are right now. Are you a top performer? Do things come easily for you? Do you have to work harder than others for results? Are you someone who always just skates by? We all have an inner thermostat that is set by how we see ourselves. And your results always correspond to what your thermostat is set at. So if you see yourself as always struggling to get new clients, then that's exactly what will happen.

If you're not sure how you see yourself, simply look at your results – they are like a lie detector test; they'll always show what your thermostat is set on. Therefore, do an analysis of your accomplishments. If you're not accomplishing much in your professional life, chances are your thermostat is set relatively low or on the negative side. If you are accomplishing a lot, are they the kind of goals that you really want and that make you happy? The more honest you can be with yourself, the more progress you'll make in the future.

Before you can *do* something, you have to first *be* something. Who do you want to be? How would someone who achieves the ultimate goal you've outlined in step one walk, talk, and behave on a daily basis? That's the person you need to become today. Stop saying and thinking phrases like, "When I get a promotion, I'll… When I get more money, I'll… When I get the job I really want, I'll…" People who think in terms of "when I get" rarely get what they want. Therefore, think as if you already have what you desire, and act accordingly. When you make the decision to be the kind of person who lives your ultimate goals, then those results will come naturally. Start today with some small changes, because small, positive changes over time lead to success.

Stop asking, "Am I able to reach this goal?" Of course you're able – you're able to do just about anything with the right training and persistence. The correct question to ask is, "Am I willing to do what it takes to reach this goal?" So many people are concerned about whether they can do something. They wonder whether they're good enough. If they believe they are unable to do something or aren't good enough, it's really because they're unwilling to do what it takes to make them able or good enough. Professional athletes are a prime example. Many people believe athletes are born with some sort of natural ability. While that may be true for a small percentage of athletes, the majority had to practice for many hours every day to get to their current skill levels – and they still practice every day to keep making improvements.

One important aspect that we found beneficial in goal setting is to celebrate even the smallest of victories. This was difficult for us at first because we were conditioned that celebrations cost money. Since we didn't have any at the time, we had to reprogram our thought process. Soon we realised that there are many activities that don't cost any money at all. We went for walks along the beach, drove into the city, or just spent time relaxing together in our home. One reward we found particularly enjoyable was to travel into the city and visit all of the beautiful hotels. We would sit in the lobby and visualize ourselves as guests having a cuppa (Australian for cup of tea). This put an image in our minds and helped us feel like guests rather than just visitors in the lobby.

The Goal of Giving

We all have talents, gifts, and uniqueness. Our obligation is to accept these gifts and spend our lives sharing our gifts with others. What are your talents? What gives you flow? How can you serve? We are here to serve – not to deserve. What value are you contributing? Doing what you love and focusing on how you can create value will bring wealth and prosperity. When you come from a place of growth and abundance, you celebrate the success of others. Their successes do not take way from your success. Competition comes from a belief that there is not enough, and that in order for me to get what I want, I must take it from someone else. Just imagine how different your professional and personal life would be if you came from a platform of abundance and believed there is enough for everyone. Some of the greatest achievements come from people working together to create a win-win situation. You earn money and abundance by helping other people to succeed and reach their goals.

Use your gifts, talents, and passion to make a difference. Ask yourself, "How can I serve?" These ideas are important to living a balanced life. Giving of our time, money, and efforts, even off the job, can often produce wonderful results for the giver. Because giving produces positive emotions in us, we are then more effective and productive in life.

Giving is extremely powerful. Just look at how much all of us like to give presents and to show others how much they mean to us. Gratitude (which we'll discuss in Chapter IX) and giving are essential to wealth and prosperity. Rediscover the joy of giving. Be kind. Every act of kindness matters. You never know what it will result in. If you are forced to choose between being kind and being right, always choose kindness. All human beings thrive when they are needed, when they can be of service, and when they can use their talents for a good cause. Just look at the massive mobilizations after natural disasters or during wartime. Part of our culture is fostering the demand to get before you can give, but it doesn't work that way. If you want more of something, you have to give it first. If you want more loyal customers, you must first render excellent customer service; if you want more wealth, you must first give to others; if you want more friends, you must first be a friend. It all starts with us. Decide right now to stop the blame game and take the focus away from yourself. What do you want more of in your life?

Ask yourself who you want to be and who you want to help. We must always love people and use money. It is never the other way around. Money just is. It's not good or bad – it just is. Money will not change you. It will just make you more of what you are – good or bad. The wants in your life are for the growth experience. While you work towards your goal, you grow and stretch. It's not because you just want to have more.

When your intention is great enough, you will always find the needed time and energy to accomplish your goals. If you find yourself having a difficult time with your goals, then your intention is not strong enough. If it is strong enough, you will find the time, resources, and solutions.

Every morning:

- Write down your goals.

- List your tasks for the day.

- Visualize the end result.

- Listen to or read something that inspires you.

Goal setting is important and leads us in the right direction professionally and personally. Be willing to change and stand out, even when it scares you. Fear exists in all humans. None of us are exempt. No one reached success doing what was comfortable.

To review:

- Where do you want to be professionally? What type of life do you want to have?

- If you want to do something, you have to be willing to stand out in a crowd.

- Be the change you want to be in the world. You can do that in your office, your community, and your family... right where you are.

- Fear exists in all humans.

- Always start goal setting with the end in mind.

- Celebrate even the smallest of accomplishments.

Chapter Questions

1. What may have stopped you from setting goals in the past?

2. In one area of your life that requires attention, write down a short-, medium-, and long-term goal.

3. For each of these goals, write down one thing that you can do in the next 24 hours to move towards this goal. If possible, tell a trusted person so that you become accountable.

4. How will you celebrate your success?

Chapter VII

Opening the Door: Letting Go and Moving On

We must be willing to let go of the life we have planned, so as to accept the life that is waiting for us.

– Joseph Campbell

The blame game – blaming anyone and everything – is a behaviour we've all been guilty of a time or two in our lives. Why do people do this? Simply because they aren't ready, or willing, to take a long hard look in the mirror at the person who is truly responsible. Looking to others rather than looking to yourself is much easier than admitting it's your fault. There is one thing that most adults fear more than death, and that is being wrong. It is this fear that prevents us, most of the time, from letting go of the old. Too many times when we are about to let go, we feel that we are admitting to having been wrong.

You see, we feel as if we have invested way too much time and energy to learn and figure out what we believe. We have, therefore, an overwhelmingly powerful emotional investment in what we think we know - our ways of doing things, our priorities, and our beliefs and feelings about people, places, and things. When we owned our bed and breakfast and finances were tight, we couldn't seem to let go. We hung on, thinking that times were going to get better. Once we came to the realization that nothing was going to change, we made the decision to let go. The moment we did so, it sold. Letting go of the old is one of the most difficult decisions for people to make. When your old, worn-out habits, routines, and feelings, ineffective thought patterns and impressions, and unhealed emotional scars get in the way of progress, it's time to let go and move on.

Before learning the value of letting go, I wallowed in misery and wasted months crying over our financial situation. I wondered why this happened to me after I've been a good person and helped others. I remember listening to one of our mentors, Bob Proctor, on one of our calls, talking about getting the results you want in life. He mentioned that if you're not getting the result you want, there is only one person you need to talk to, and he or she is always available. When he said this, I sat straight up and thought to myself, He's right. On many following phone calls, he repeated this, and the more I heard it, the more profound the message became. I finally decided to look at myself and ask what was about me that I needed to change. This one action helped me to move on to the life I never thought could be mine.

– Geraldine

The reason why many people don't achieve the success they deserve is simple; they refuse to let go and move forward. Far too many people focus so intently on the past that they miss out on chances that will affect their future. To let go also means letting go of your ego. As we mentioned earlier, no one wants to admit being wrong, but until you are able to do so with an open and honest heart, you'll have a difficult time moving forward.

Living within the Law

As the laws of our mechanical universe exist, so do the laws of our existence. We've talked a good deal about the Law of Attraction and how you attract your thoughts into your life. There are actually many more universal laws beyond the Law of Attraction. Many people doubt the existence of some of these, but let us ask you one question: Do you doubt the Law of Gravity? No; you know that what goes up must come down. So why is it so easy to doubt the rest of the universal laws? Many doubt because they can't actually see them. Well, you can't actually see electricity, but you know that flipping a switch turns on the light. These laws aren't to be questioned.

Everything in our universe is governed by unwavering laws. As you understand the importance of living in harmony with these laws, you'll soon find fulfilment not just in your finances and relationships, but in all areas of your life. The universal laws are all interconnected and based on the fact that everything in the universe is energy. At the microscopic level, we are nothing more than globs of electrons spinning fervently. Once we act in accordance with these laws, our physical, mental, spiritual, and emotional growth flourishes because we're following the flow of the currents that build and maintain all of creation.

Since all of our thoughts, feelings, words, and actions are forms of energy, they vibrate back to us to create our realities. Energy moves in a circle, so the combined thoughts, feelings, words, and actions of everyone on the planet create our collective consciousness. In order to create a world of prosperity and abundance for our entire universe, it is essential to alter our thoughts and emotions.

The law is the law, and your being believes it. It already knows, so it does not look for understanding beyond what it knows on a rational, conscious level, and we will tell you that your knowingness does not come from your mind. There is only one way to correct errors in thinking, and that is to provide detailed outlines of how (the same how that the rational mind desires) this works, how they (universal laws) always work, and exactly how to use them. For this is what we see is missing for you and for humanity. Now remember, you are the scientist, and the world is your lab. You need only learn the laws that will unlock the ability to connect with it in a way that works all the time, every time. There are several other universal laws as well, and we strongly encourage you to learn about them and live your life accordingly. One of the books that really helped us was *Working with the Law* by Raymond Holliwell. We, however, would like to expand on just a few of the universal laws that have been so beneficial in our lives.

The Law of Forgiveness

Are you still letting the things you and others have done influence your life? One of the best definitions we have heard is that refusing to forgive someone, regardless of what they have done to you, is like taking poison and expecting the other person to die. The people who have hurt you are not spending a second thinking about it or dwelling on it. But you relive it over and over again and keep it as an open wound inside of you, poisoning your own life. Forgiveness is easy once you stop dwelling on the injustices or perceived injustices done to you by someone else. As these negative thoughts invade your mind, practice replacing them with good ones. You'll soon find they rarely come into your conscious thoughts and are then no big deal. Then, true forgiveness occurs naturally. Soon you can see them as a silly part of your past or, even better, a lesson from which you grew and overcame pettiness or resentment.

Why is there a need to forgive? The lack of forgiveness creates grief, despair, resentment, and anger within the mind and skews your perception of what's really true. This in turn leads you to make assumptions and decisions based on false ideas and creates unhappiness and lack of fulfilment within your life. The wound is an incomplete energetic cycle and, if left unresolved, it infiltrates our other relationships and situations and can eventually manifest as physical illness and disease.

The art of forgiveness gives us a possibility to grow. The Dalai Lama sees the Chinese Government as his "secret friend", allowing him to show unconditional love and grow despite their persecution of himself and his followers. He is literally in exile from his homeland, Tibet, of which he is considered not only the spiritual leader and authority, but also the rightful temporal, or earthly, ruler. The Dalai Lama has a great capacity to forgive, and his teachings are always profound on the matters of goodness, and the fair, loving treatment of humans, no matter which path they are following. His capacity to love is great, and emulating his forgiveness is a great way to find forgiveness for yourself and to practice it toward others. When we let go of our resentments, we heal and become better human beings. This is a great step for living according to your purpose in life.

By letting go, you heal the wound. Often it is the things we have done that cause the most pain: people we have hurt, bad choices we made, or just negative thoughts we've held about ourselves and others. These only serve to sabotage our entire lives and the results we get. We have spent numerous hours beating ourselves up over some wrong choices and for some things we realised we had done to cause others pain, whether intentionally or not. We are so tough on ourselves. Often when we make big, bold decisions, the little voice in our heads reminds us of all the times we've failed, and we jump back into safety. We revert to blaming someone else, a situation, or even worse, ourselves! Stop playing the blame game. Forgive and move forward.

It was absolutely liberating for us when we realised that the things that have happened in our lives, the things we have said and done, have brought us to the place we are today. And by forgiving ourselves for past actions, we freed up so much space and energy for the goals we wanted to achieve. Be grateful for your experiences. Learn from them and move forward with increased knowledge – especially the knowledge that forgiveness matters and can be a wonderful tool for moving forward. When we forgive, the universe opens up new more profound and loving experiences.

We once heard someone say that you will repeat the bad things in your life until you have learned from them. Only then are you ready to move forward. Emerson said, "Every soul has to learn the whole lesson for itself." We truly believe this. Have you ever noticed that you often get similar situations or reactions occurring at the same time in your life? Maybe you have conflicts with friends or co-workers where it seems everyone is against you. Take the time when this occurs to see what your role is in it and what lesson needs to be learned. Are you failing to forgive, or simply blaming others for the apparent chaos? Your energy is getting sucked up in all of the drama. Often, we let it drag us further into the destruction, versus seeing what we can do to take responsibility and resolve the issues and conflict. It can often be as simple as saying, "I was wrong. I am sorry."

Imagine waking up one morning and feeling a glow about you. Burdens of the past have been lifted, and the heaviness of your heart has been lightened. You no longer are filled with pain, grief, anger, or resentment, and your spirit feels free to live once again. Through the Law of Forgiveness, the gates open to a new world for us. Once we've truly forgiven – not only others, but ourselves as well – we can fully embrace life and all that it has to offer.

The Law of Compensation

The Law of Compensation is not specifically referring to money. As the Byrds say in "Turn! Turn! Turn!", "To every thing there is a season, and a time to every purpose under heaven." For everything you lose in life, you gain something else. We cannot have successes without failures or hardships without gains. This law of nature is about balance, harmony, and equilibrium. Think of it this way: Have you ever had a time in your life when you lost something very dear to you, only to find something better to replace it? We lost our bed and breakfast but gained Teggelove Mentoring and Coaching.

Once we understand that for every gain there is a loss, we can free ourselves from envy and live contentedly. There is a time for contentment and a time for discontentment. When we use our challenges to raise ourselves to a higher level, we are living in line with the Law of Compensation. There is no gain without loss: no gain without pain. Our success depends not on what we take up, but what we give up. So we willingly sacrifice time and comfort to reach our goals. And if we experience a temporary setback, we're not discouraged because we understand that hidden in our problems are opportunities waiting to be uncovered.

The Law of Non-resistance

The Law of Non-resistance states, "What you resist persists." The more you dislike a certain thing, the more difficult it will be to remove it from your life. You may be in a situation you hate and that you are resisting, not realizing that it is this very resistance that is keeping you stuck and preventing you from moving forward in your life.

Until you stop resisting, the negative situation will persist. Where you are right now is a result of your past thoughts, feelings, and actions. And when you resist this present state, you are giving energy to it. As Ralph Waldo Emerson said, "The only thing that grows is that which you give energy to." Take some time to think of the negative, disempowering thoughts you say to yourself. Are any of these familiar?

- I'll never be successful.

- I'll never have enough money.

- My life is such a disappointment.

- I'm not good enough.

When you are in a state of resistance, your mind and body are engaged in a conflict. There is a tremendous inner struggle. Any positive thoughts you have or affirmations you may say are countered and neutralized by these negative, resisting thoughts. Your life will not improve until you improve the quality of your thinking.

I had made the decision to stop allowing negative thoughts to enter my mind and focus only on the positives in life. One day during class, one of my students raised her hand and asked me why I was so happy all of the time. I had only seen this young lady on six or seven occasions with this class. My response to her was, "Thank you for the comment. That was the evidence I was looking for." This young lady had only been around me once a week for a little over a month, yet she could see my positive attitude. I knew at that moment how powerful it can be to change your thoughts.

– Bill

Living according to the Law of Non-resistance makes you calmer, more focused, and confident about achieving your goals and dreams. You no longer waste your precious mental energy fighting your current life. Instead, you will find a way to positively deal with whatever challenges come your way and use them as stepping stones to a better life and a better you.

The Law of Giving and Receiving

We are only entrusted with our possessions. It is not *my* home, *my* car, or *my* money. We can only give what we have been entrusted with. What we do not have is not ours to give. We can only give in accordance with the means that universe has entrusted to us. Many people, usually in response to an emotional plea, have gone out to a lending institution, borrowed money, and gone into personal debt in order to give to what they considered to be a worthy cause.

If we believe that through the world in which we live, the universe both meets our needs and gives us all things to enjoy, we are accountable for how we use our resources. How do we use our money or talents to show our gratitude? In the act of self-giving, we experience extraordinary grace to remould our innermost beings and release our potential. As we recognize the generosity of our universal gifts, our needs are met and we're sustained. Much of everyday life is determined by economics and personal income. The use of our gifts is a profoundly important and practical demonstration of our faith and trust in the infinite intelligence. And the way we use our money and resources is a significant sign of our concern for the universe and an expression of our love.

At the core of our beings, each of us is a vehicle through which the energy of the universe manifests. This flow of energy never stops. If it did, we would disintegrate instantly. This may be difficult for some to understand. Think of a space shuttle returning to the earth's atmosphere. The energy created by the shuttle's mass and speed must be released during re-entry. The space shuttle slows down through a series of S-shaped turns and the manipulation of friction between the atmosphere and the craft, creating a tremendous amount of heat. A portion of this heat can be absorbed, but the rest must be deflected. If not, the craft will disintegrate upon re-entry. As a side note, re-entry is an excellent example of energy being changed from one form to another. We are always receiving an abundance of love and prosperity, perfect health, perfect vocation, perfect relationships, and intuitive guidance. So why don't we know this? Why don't we experience all of these wonderful possibilities in our lives?

Just as the shuttle's re-entry will be halted if the energy flow is disrupted, when we break the Law of Giving and Receiving, we interrupt the stream of life's energy by neglecting to give as we receive. Each of us has a direct connection to God and to our abundant supply. We adhere to the universal laws as we allow the universe to express itself through us. Because we've become disconnected with the Law of Giving and Receiving, we've created barriers to the universal energy readily available to us. We repeatedly look outside of ourselves to find the answers to our needs and desires and ignore this limitless supply. How can we break through these barriers?

Stop living according to the laws of the physical plane. All of us want to prosper economically. The physical-plane laws teach us that we must work for everything we have. When we live according to these laws, we work for a set amount, which may or may not meet the needs of ourselves and families. The universal laws, on the other hand, promise overflowing prosperity and abundance as we give.

Give with a positive attitude. If you give out of guilt or empathy, you may as well have not given at all. We receive as we give only if we do so without reluctance or resentment. The universe provides you with everything you need, so that you can share with others.

Let go. Give with the expectation of getting nothing in return. You can't drop off a box of old clothes at the Salvos and then go and buy a lottery ticket, expecting to walk away a millionaire. Sorry, folks; it doesn't work that way. Your generosity will be returned, but it will be in the universe's time, not yours. God rewards you through avenues you never knew existed. Abundance is unlimited and comes into our lives through undreamed of channels. Don't be afraid to give, because the universe will supply you with all you need.

The Art of Allowing

Before you can begin any exploration into self-improvement, you need to consider what you are not doing as well as you could be. This is not a judgment or a time to criticize yourself. It is a time to examine the way you interact with your current life. Are you negative about the good in your life? Do you find yourself expecting the worst to happen? If so, it's time to write down these behaviours as you notice them so that you can begin to figure out ways to change your actions and reactions.

Most people don't realise that we must also stop resisting the ability to accept good into our lives. We are brought up to give and taught that giving is good. But we need to learn how to accept the good into our lives, too. Giving and receiving go hand in hand. How well do you accept compliments? Do you feel embarrassed when you receive a gift?

Just think of your desire and leave it out there. Go away, and trust that your life will be filled with abundance. Sadly, many people give up just a couple of steps before the finish line because they've decided that if it's not working by now, it's never going to work at all. Worse still are those who throw in more and more energy because they think that with more resources, the results will come faster.

Everything in this world has a natural development time, and this fact will not change no matter what resources you throw at a situation. So relax and be patient. Remember that as part of the universe, you are also governed by its laws, and you cannot change the natural development time.

With so many places for people to get help these days, there's no need for people to hang on to a life that no longer suits them and drags them down. For us, part of the letting-go process was to work with a life coach. This is particularly difficult for those in our generation, the baby boomers. We were raised with many limiting beliefs about money, spirituality, and relationships. As we mature, they become so ingrained that many of us think that we can't change. This was true for us, so we sought the assistance of a life coach to help us through. As the saying goes, "Nothing changes if nothing changes." Once we were able to free our minds of these ridiculous limiting beliefs, our lives began to unfold in an amazing way – so much that we wanted to take our experiences and help others see their own potential as well. This is why we felt destined to form Teggelove Mentoring and Coaching (www.flightplanprogram.com). Through this, we've been able to give others the freedom that we achieved and watch them soar on eagle's wings alongside us.

You might be upset about things that have happened in the past, things that may truly have been someone else's fault. Or they may have been your fault. In either case, you need to begin to let go before you can move forward. Allow yourself to feel what your life would be like and to receive all the goodness in it. For most of us, the past is something that we truly believe we cannot change. What you need to do, however, is to begin looking at your past as something that can be changed in your mind. For example, if you are upset about a dream that you missed out on in the past, start looking at what you could have done differently. And then you can take those lessons into your next dream plans, making them a positive part of your new life.

You are the one with the ability to move forward into the life you deserve and the life that you want. But instead of being held down by the chains and the weight of your past, you need to let go and move forward. When this weight is off your shoulders, you will find that you can soar higher toward your goals than ever before.

Chapter Questions

1. In relation to your major challenge in life, what do you need to let go of?

2. Who or what have you been blaming?

3. Identify your self-talk. Is it positive or negative?

Chapter VIII

Nothing Is Ever As It Seems: Perceptions

Any fact facing us is not as important as our attitude
toward it, for that determines our success or failure. The
way you think about a fact may defeat you before you
ever do anything about it. You are overcome by the fact
because you think you are.

– Norman Vincent Peale

When we were going through the worst financial crash in our
history, no one knew it. As a matter of fact, most people who knew
of us thought we were quite wealthy. At that point in time, status
was important to us, even though we would never admit it. We
now see status as spending money that you don't have on things
that you don't need in order to impress people you don't really
know or don't really like. This has become a huge social problem
and is one of the main contributors to credit card debt.

Our families and friends were also oblivious to our financial
situation because we kept it covered up. It wasn't until we told
them about our problems that they found out. Nobody could
believe it. We would hear statements such as, "But you both looked
so happy" or "We would never have guessed anything was wrong."
As with everything else in life, nothing is ever as it seems.

The way in which we believe, feel, act, think, and speak in relation to ourselves and others is our attitude. How is yours? Do you wake up each morning excited to face the day? Or do you hit the snooze button several times because you just don't want to deal with it? Stop for a moment and think about your thoughts and words. What do you expect to happen each day? What are your expectations for your business, relationships, or life? Do they match your outcomes?

The Law of Attraction is a fundamental universal law and has the ability to transform our lives. Many have heard of this law but don't truly understand its underlying principle and power. This law states that all your thoughts, mental images, and the emotions attached to them will manifest into your reality. Basically, like attracts like, and all that you have in life has been attracted to you by your thoughts. Every day you attract situations, events, circumstances, and people into your life by your predominant thoughts. Based on this information, how important do you think attitude is to your life?

The attitude we carry throughout the day is paramount if the Law of Attraction is to work in our favour. So how is yours? Limitless or limited? If you want to have a positive attitude, it is vital that all of your thoughts are constructive and encouraging. This may seem like an impossible feat in today's society, with all of the negativity in the media and on the Internet. When you watch TV, read the newspapers, or surf the Internet, do so with the knowledge that every destructive word or harmful image has an adverse impact on your attitude.

Your attitude has tremendous power and can infiltrate every part of your life as well as those around you. If you have an upbeat and optimistic attitude, others want to spend time in your presence. The physical benefits of a positive attitude are infinite as well. Your perception influences your overall health. Research, for example, has shown that people who have a good outlook on life are in better health and may even live longer than those who don't. For instance, a Dutch study found that optimists had less risk of any cause of death than those who admitted to having a pessimistic view of life. Less stress and increased energy are two additional advantages. If you want to feel better both physically and emotionally, make certain to engage only in activities, behaviours, and conversations that fill your life with positive stimuli.

A Purposeful Attitude

If a positive attitude is so important for your entire life, why do so many people have negative attitudes? One of the primary reasons why so many have a pessimistic viewpoint is that they aren't living according to their purpose. If you could take an honest look at your life, what would you see? A life you have carefully crafted? Or does your life reflect what others expect of you? Are you living according to the expectations of your parents, siblings, spouse, or friends? Perhaps this is the reason you've felt incomplete and as if your life is lacking something. Maybe you're living someone else's purpose and not your own.

Each of us should live in the way that suits us best. Otherwise, how can we maintain a positive attitude toward life? So often we are expected to act in certain ways or do certain things. How many times have you heard statements such as "That's not right" or "You can't do that"? Even today there is a lingering belief that we should act according to others' expectations. This causes us to live in a manner inconsistent with who we truly are. If you aren't living according to your purpose, you simply aren't living.

It is difficult if not impossible to maintain a positive attitude when you're constantly trying to please everyone else. Do you feel the need to change your convictions, stances, or beliefs just to fit in? Don't lose yourself to another person. You need to have the confidence to express your opinions and the courage to stand your ground. To find your purpose, explore your own beliefs and values and what they mean to you. This process of self-discovery brings you closer to your authentic self and to your passion.

Once you uncover your passion, you develop a zest for life evident through your attitude. All of a sudden, your willpower and stamina increase, and you're more productive. Life isn't meant for us to just exist, and it certainly shouldn't be a chore. We need to thrive and enjoy every moment on earth. Knowing that you are living your life on your terms and making a difference in the world is energizing. Once your attitude is reinforced with passion, your actions, thoughts, and words become a driving force behind your purpose in life.

We all have a passion for something, and while some passions are grandiose, others are small and important only in the eye of the beholder. All that truly matters is that you discover and follow yours with an unwavering commitment. Passion isn't easily hidden. When you are passionate, your attitude of confidence and self-assurance and your belief that anything is possible inspires others to find the true meaning of their own lives. Purpose fuelled by passion gives you a belief in yourself and the positive attitude to reach every goal and achieve unlimited success in whatever you desire.

Look to the Future

We should live in the present moment, not allowing any events or circumstances from our pasts to inhibit us. Your future begins with now. One of the main reasons that many of us do not achieve the level of success we desire is because we are constantly dwelling on history. Instead, learn from your mistakes and move on. Every moment we live in the present is an opportunity to harvest the lessons from the past and plant new seeds for the future. We cannot hold grudges or think back to yesterday. It is important to remove ourselves from our old belief systems and live in the Now. If you live in the past, you won't be able to look to the future because your mindset will not change.

As the world evolves, we all need to follow our own courses. Our roles in society are changing rapidly and, with many of us rising to the top of the corporate ladder, starting our own businesses, and taking on more leadership positions, we need to look to the future. We are visionaries. As a visionary, you have the power to create a better world not only for yourself but for others as well. Vision awakens our creativity and imagination and empowers us to pursue endeavors once thought impossible. Visionaries don't listen to voices of doubt and warnings of possible failure; they forge their own paths, no matter how difficult.

Living your life with this attitude creates a momentum which enables you to break through boundaries and barriers. Success in any form is accompanied by a vision. A visionary is not someone who is gifted or talented. Visionaries are people who decide to live their lives as their own and inspire other individuals to do the same. Most choose to follow others and ignore what they want out of life. Visionaries, however, listen to their inner voices and live according to their own beliefs, values, and ideals.

A young man was riding on a crowded bus one day and wondered what would happen if the bus could travel at the speed of light. This one thought soon became Albert Einstein's theory of relativity. He once said, "In the middle of difficulty lies opportunity." He was one of the world's greatest visionaries. You can't go through life with the attitude that every challenge or obstacle is detrimental. What will set you apart from others is your ability to transform the stumbling blocks in your life into opportunities. As you read through the chapters in *Beyond Broke*, notice that one of the common threads is that we have all had setbacks and struggled with limiting beliefs. Why is it that so many people choose to make excuses and blame any problem for their circumstance in life? Remember, it is the decisions you make in life, not the events that help create your future.

What happens when situations don't turn out as you had hoped? Do you fall back on gloom-and-doom thinking? Believe the absolute worst is going to happen? Or do you take a step back, regain your composure, and tell yourself everything is going to be all right? According to the Law of Attraction, each time you expect something bad to happen, it does. This is why it is so crucial to eliminate the negative and build and focus on the positives. What sort of stories do you tell yourself when events don't go as planned? Many times our tendency is to revert to sabotaging thoughts. Thinking in this sort of way is fairly common. So it's difficult to believe that being positive is our innate nature because we have learned this negativity from those around us. Your true positive nature emerges from within only with focused effort. We habitually derive a negative attitude because we live in a negative world and must deal with negative people. When we let negative thoughts enter our minds and leave our mouths, we're robbing ourselves of great possibilities. What matters is if we have the commitment to shift our thought process to a more positive and productive one.

Once you change your perception and view challenges as opportunities, you not only gain the ability to conquer them, you enhance your chances of success as well. Worry and stress leave your mind and free you to think of more creative solutions. Our true characters are revealed when we face adversity and, depending on how crisis situations are handled, we succeed or fail. The average person's mindset is conditioned to think in terms of safety and comfort zones. With this thought process, you have a low tolerance for stressful situations and more than likely don't accomplish your goals.

In life, there is no such thing as safety, and change is inevitable. The most successful individuals thrive on adversity and leverage it for future achievements. Two essential qualities for visionaries are a strong self-image and an optimistic attitude. Without these, you fall prey to the opinions and criticisms of others. Conventional thinking is mediocre and doesn't equate with success. To fulfil any desire you have in life, you need to have a vision, possess unshakeable confidence, and learn to listen to your inner guidance.

With family, job, community activities, networking, and trying to squeeze in a little "me" time at the end of the day, we can feel a bit overwhelmed. An optimistic outlook is essential. It not only makes life better for us, but also for those around us. There are many ways we can bring positivity into our lives instead of focusing on the negative. Always look for your strengths, whatever the situation. Make every attempt to find the good, and make the most out of all situations, even if the situation isn't one that you would like to be in.

If negative situations appear, you must use your will and refuse to lower yourself to negative thoughts, words, actions, and emotions. Decide not only to focus on the positive, but to promote encouraging thoughts, words, and actions throughout the rest of your day as well. No matter what, stay positive – even when you have the feeling that the whole world is against you and you're losing momentum. It takes determination, strength, faith, and the power of your will to focus on the positive when intense negativity descends. As you focus more on the positive, think of the positive, speak of the positive, and take positive and good actions, your mindset will soon follow. Suddenly you will look around and find that the negativity has gone and your day has been filled with goodness and joy.

Take the time to learn this skill, and you will see that in time you can easily let go of the negative emotions in your life and fill your mind with only healthy ones. Maintaining a positive attitude is 80 per cent mindset. The other 20 per cent depends on your willingness to change. Focusing on the positives in your life makes you resilient, and building optimism is a key aspect of success in life.

It is important that we practice focusing on our strengths and fostering a positive attitude. This leads to productive habits in the future. As we all know, this is contagious. We want to pass this mindset on to others so they feel empowered and confident as well. Thinking that your abilities are limitless and success is inevitable inspires others and transforms your life for the better. Encouraging words, behaviours, and thoughts bring a sense of security and improved self-esteem, which helps to build your positive outlook. So if you want to change your life, you need to change yourself. You need to change your attitude.

When we are dealing with the physical world, we must look into the importance of perception. None of us would go to work only wearing shoes, or buy a car without an engine. But many of us look at our lives and get the wrong perception or see only a portion of the truth. To some, a wooden box is a piece of art; to others, it is a nothing more than a storage bin. Mental realities are very much like physical realities in that they are more accurately and completely understood when you view them from the correct perception. Once we realise our positions, we are able to conceive our perceptions of life. It is here that we are able to clearly see if we need to shift or adjust our individual perceptions. This gives us clarity on our problems and solutions.

It is difficult for us to gain insight if we are only looking in one direction. By understanding our authentic selves, we are then able to understand our actions. We must understand our physical and emotional reactions. The ability to step into your own skin opens you to unlimited possibilities in life. Your future is yours to bend and shape through the understanding of perceptions and decisions.

Make the Choice

The best technique to change your perception is to make the correct choices. The more choices we have, the better we are able to see ourselves for who we really are. We can stumble through life thinking we have no choices and that we are imprisoned by others who control us. *They* make us act a certain way. *They* keep us from becoming all that we can be. Just who are *they*? Contrary to this way of thinking and reacting, we have infinite possibilities at our disposal. Believe it or not, these treasures are just waiting for you to pick them up. Your imprisonment is of your own making. *They* don't keep you there. *You* do!

With the right help and direction, you can achieve any goal you desire. The choices we make determine our future. With this thought process, your struggles and frustrations become possibilities, not obstacles.

First, we have a choice as to how we react to any situation. It can rule us, or we can take charge of our own lives. Many of us go through our entire lives doing nothing but reacting to stimuli from our surroundings and other people. We choose to stay in a place of victimisation and blame everyone around us for our circumstances. Make a conscious choice to become proactive. Instead of waiting for someone to tell you what you need to fix, take action on your own and realise that you are perfect the way you are. Take responsibility for your own thoughts and actions. Your perceptions should be reflected in your actions.

We can all find excuses not to change or not to act. Have you ever thought about what's behind your excuses? That is, have you pondered what is truly behind your beliefs about lacking the time or the capacity to do something great? Those are excuses that we've developed to cope with so-called everyday life. We tend to either live in the past, struggle in the present, or look anxiously to the future. We detach ourselves from the Now, the greatest truth, and its ability to encompass everything in the world as it exists this very moment.

Do you know what we do instead? We carry with us a pocket full of excuses that robs us of our ability to be fully aware and do great things. In those excuses we find brilliant, believable explanations for why we cannot do the things we want to do. Whenever we choose, we can dip into that pocket, pull out an excuse, and sit down on our couches, ignoring the Now in favour of so-called comfort. We rearrange some pillows and sink in, watching the clock in anticipation of a potential brief moment of future fun. Or we find ourselves pacing before the very same sofas with a systematic tension in our bodies – five steps forward, a quick turn, four steps back, and a brief pause.

We look around for some time to do the things we didn't get done already because we were busy pacing, because we were caught in the stress that removes us from the Now. We spend most of our time with our heads in the excuse pocket, far from being present in the Now. We all have a great ability to be creative, and when it comes to creating excuses we are fabulous. It is time to cut a hole in your pocket and let the excuses escape.

Your choices can be purposeful and intentional. If you are a constant victim, it is because you choose to be one; you like others to feel sorry for you. The responsibility is placed on others. When we hit our lowest points in life, it's the time to make a choice. Choose your future. You can either continue to sink further into that dark, slick pocket, or find something to pull yourself out of it. This decision will take you toward the first steps of your journey to a new perception.

Strong decisions are driven by intent. If we say one thing and do another, then we never really intended to do it anyway. Not in our heart of hearts. Intent can be a noun, but to change anything it needs to become a verb. It includes a goal that you set for yourself, focusing on it, and working towards reaching it. See yourself reach for what you want, and see yourself achieve it. The dictionary defines intent as aspiring to, labouring for, setting one's eyes on, dreaming of, and taking upon oneself. These all start internally. You have to make the choice for yourself.

You might ask yourself, "What about all the times I fail?" Look at it through different glasses. Take the lesson. We learn more through our mistakes than our achievements. However, this is not to take away from reaching your goal or obtaining your dream. It feels great. Enjoy it. Trust yourself. We grow from every experience. Believe that nothing is impossible if you choose with intent. When we don't trust ourselves or stay focused on what we want out of this life that is positive and good, we delay our rewards.

Look at all of your alternatives. Decide which one serves you best. We allow ourselves to be led from one thing to another. All of us have days when we know exactly what we are going to accomplish before dinner – then a random thought sends us on a rabbit trail in a dark forest. We see something that needs attention and turn to take care of it. Next, we uncover another minor task while doing the first. It goes on and on. Suddenly it's five o'clock and we haven't even started on the main project we wanted to finish.

You don't want to become so set in your plan that you can't address emergencies or others who need your help, but you need to use self-control. Don't lose focus. Our conscious minds think everything through that we are aware of, and then make a choice based on our information, as well as our feelings, which originate in our subconscious. We use the filter in our brains to allow and accept certain information as part of the decision-making process.

Let's look at opposites for a few minutes. We look at our choices as good or bad. We think that someone is ugly or beautiful. If we go all the way back to our senses, we taste things as sweet or sour. These are all opposites. If we concentrate on the negative side of every choice, then that's what we choose. Train your mind to realise that you are good. Life is about limitations or possibilities. Push yourself to make the choices that are positive. Refuse to be negative. Choose to have a positive way of looking at life and your circumstances, and choose to make them better.

When you aren't sure what your choices are, it could be as simple as deciding to keep your good attitude and look at the world from that viewpoint. From there you can attract positive thoughts, people, tools, and experiences to help you progress along your path. Remember to think in possibilities and not limit yourself in the choices you make. Don't make a choice based on other people's doubts. What others think is unreasonable is not necessarily so. If you let others make your choices for you, it is like disconnecting from the Internet. The experience is disconnecting you from yourself and what you really want in life. If you take the easy way out and just give in to what others think, you won't be able to realise your full potential. Make the choice that is good for you, and it will bring you the abundance you deserve.

Once you make your decision and know your purpose, there will be small course corrections along your path, as we talked about earlier, but your focus will stay the same. It is with commitment to your choice that you build your character. It moves you to action and keeps you positive. It's like the difference between a rabbit and a sheep. The rabbit is totally committed when it is part of a fur coat, but the sheep is only invested. His coat has been cut off and made into wool material for a winter coat, but the sheep will grow more wool.

The choice to change your perception unlocks your imagination and creativity. It pulls you out of the pocket. Those thoughts build an image and grow into the reality that you created yourself. You didn't have to wait for somebody else to come along and tell you what to do or how to do it. You don't have to depend on someone else to make your choices for you anymore. You have the power inside of you and the confidence to make the choices you need to make.

Many of us don't make choices to help us find who we are because it removes us from our comfort zones. Living in our comfort zones is rather natural and expected. We don't get anxious when we are with the familiar, the comfortable. We feel secure in repetitive behaviours and, unless challenged, most of us have neither reason nor desire to step outside our comfort zones. Because of our anxiety about the new, we prefer to sit on a thorn rather than change. The new is too difficult to face. We convince ourselves internally that we cannot handle doing something unusual.

Comfort zones also become pockets full of excuses because we're concerned about acceptance from others. If we do something out of the ordinary, what will our friends and colleagues think about us? We are all conditioned to believe we cannot live without approval from others. Most of us stay within our defined comfort zones so we do not have to risk losing the approval of others.

Comfort zones tend to create complacency. You feel secure within your imaginary boundaries and don't take the time to look at the opportunity to step outside those lines. You're comfortable there; why should you go to a place where you are uncomfortable? So how do you take a look at your comfort zone and decide to step out? First, you need to know that highly successful people step out of their comfort zones with regularity. They identify goals they want to achieve and then adapt new and different behaviour patterns to reach those goals. If you decide to try to step outside your comfort zone, take it easy on yourself and take just one or two steps at a time. A gigantic leap off a mountain is not necessary.

You are just wonderful as you are! You are amazing; don't you remember? It's just a shame the world doesn't get to see all of you and that you don't fully realise exactly how wonderful you are yet.

It is now the moment for an important change of perception…

Chapter Questions

1. What are your perceptions about money?

2. In what way have you been conditioned by family, friends, the media, and society in general?

3. Of your responses to the two questions above, which ones would you like to change?

4. Recall a situation, whether current or past, where things are or were not going as well as you would like. Now identify three *positives* in this situation.

Chapter IX

For All in Life: Gratitude

Gratitude is not only the greatest of virtues, but the parent of all the others.

– Cicero

The topic of this chapter is difficult for us to put on paper because it is such an emotional one. Gratitude has had such an enormous impact on our lives. We are grateful for not only the good in our lives, but the bad as well. This goes back to the Law of Compensation we discussed in an earlier chapter. By extending gratitude during a crisis, it grows on you and becomes more profound. Expressing gratitude sends an invitation for an increased flow of energy to come into our lives, as well as generating a feeling of worthiness. As we look at the world around us, our normal tendency is to see it as it appears to be instead of seeing it as it could be. The important aspect for us to realise is that this is not just a matter of our own personal perspectives; it actually determines the kind of life and world we create going forward. Seeing the world as one with limited options is depressing and empty. However, the world looks very different when we view it through the eyes of gratitude and thanksgiving.

When we are deeply grateful for every little thing that happens around us, every moment of our lives becomes precious.

I am so grateful for all in my life: Bill, my mentors, challenges, books, songs, and music. Each one of them has had an impact on my life in a profound way.

– Geraldine

We had many wonderful and giving mentors in our life who were willing to share their knowledge with us. How grateful are we for them? There are not enough words to express our gratitude. With some of them it was just a word they said or a hug to help us get through our bad times. Their encouragement helped us take another step forward. And now we are grateful for the opportunity to improve other people's lives through Teggelove Mentoring and Coaching. Recognizing the presence of the energy flowing through us all the time causes us to open our hearts. This starts with gratitude. Once you begin to experience the joy of gratitude, you become more willing to give. We give so that others may find happiness within themselves. And the more we give, the more is returned to us, multiplied abundantly.

We composed a gratitude prayer which we say each day, and we would like to share this with you.

I greet this day with love and gratitude for all that I am in this present moment.

I am so grateful for all of God's love, guidance, prosperity, and abundance.

I am so grateful for my unique gifts and talents; grateful for my challenges and struggles; and so grateful for all the opportunities I have today to give, to serve, and to receive.

I am so grateful for the power I have within me that I now use to create my amazing day.

Our daughter Elissa has also incorporated a daily practice of gratitude within her family life. Every night before dinner, each member of the family takes turns stating one thing in life that they're grateful for. This is a wonderful practice because it has instilled a sense of gratitude in the children.

As we practice giving purely from the heart, and as we practice receiving with gratitude, knowing that our gratitude is a gift both to ourselves and to the giver, our egos will begin to fall away, and we will begin living, loving, and sharing from a higher state of consciousness. The concept of thankfulness suggests a state of completion. The subconscious mind does not know about time; giving thanks for any passionate dream tells the subconscious mind that the passionate dream is here now. When we thank someone for something in our day-to-day lives, such as when we receive a gift, it is usually because we have possession of the gift now. This flow of receiving followed by thankfulness is already a program that exists in our subconscious minds. Stimulating this existing program greatly accelerates the manifestation of the passionate dreams we are giving our thoughts to.

A gratitude journal is the first step to bringing simplicity, order, harmony, beauty, and joy into your life. We write five items in our journal every evening. We also make it a point to ensure that they are different. Writing your blessings in life every day puts them in your awareness and makes you much more appreciative of even the least of blessings. Consciously giving thanks each day for the abundance that exists in your life sets in motion the universal Law of Gratitude, and the more you have and are grateful for, the more you will receive in life. Use the space below to list all that you are grateful for in your life.

I'm so happy and grateful for:

Continue to journal in a separate notebook. As the months pass and you fill your journal with blessings, an inner shift in your reality will occur. Soon you will be delighted to discover how content and hopeful you are feeling. As you focus on the abundance rather than on the lack in your life, you will be increasing the abundance in your life as well as in the lives of others. This sense of fulfilment is gratitude at work, transforming your dreams into reality.

If we take the time to revisit the stick figure in Chapter IV and the Law of Forgiveness in Chapter VII, we'll see that combining gratitude with forgiveness is a powerful tool because it enables us to remove the negatives and limiting beliefs in our subconscious minds. Sandy Forster, in her book *How to be Wildly Wealthy FAST*, tells how she writes the words "thank you" on the back of her cheques as she pays her bills. This was a real eye-opener for us because we've always thought of bills as negative. But now we really do appreciate the fact that we have access to so many services in our home, and the fact that we've got the money to pay for these. Listed below are a few more gratitude affirmations from some of the authors and mentors we've had the privilege of learning from:

- I am so happy and grateful now that money comes to me in ever-increasing quantities, through multiple sources on a continuous basis. – Bob Proctor

- I love and approve of myself. – Louise Hay

- I am now a money magnet. – Dr John Demartini

- I am worthy of all the abundance and prosperity this universe has to offer. – Catherine Ponder

Affirmations

You have probably heard of affirmations before, and perhaps even used them in an effort to improve your life. Perhaps you tried to lose weight, quit smoking, or increase your self-confidence by uttering a magical phrase that was supposed to fill you with feelings of empowerment and determination. How did that work out for you? If you're like most people, you probably abandoned your practice of affirmations after a few days because you weren't seeing results.

Affirmations can have a transformative effect on your life and your goals – but only if you use them correctly. Without the proper use of affirmations, you may find yourself going around in circles, getting more frustrated by the moment. Affirmations are defined as positive declarations, statements, or judgments. When you state an affirmation, you declare that statement to be true. There are three common mistakes that you may be making in your affirmations that can slow down the process of your success.

The first mistake is not spending enough time finding out what you really want. If you walked into a pub, sat down at a table, and told the waitress you'd like "something cold", what would she say? She'd likely hand you a menu, recite the daily drink specials, and then wait for you to make a decision. It's not her job to decide what you should drink – nor is it the universe's job to decide what you want in your life.

However, many people, for a whole host of reasons, have trouble defining what they truly want. They've lived for so long with less than they deserve because of duty or religious beliefs or self-worth issues that it is hard to define what they want for themselves. If you're one of those people, know right now that it is okay to want prosperity, abundance, and happiness for yourself! Many people shy away from getting clear about what they want because they fear being disappointed when they don't get it. Guess what? If you never decide what it is that you want, you won't get it, either!

To clearly define what you want, first look at the things that you don't want in your life. Start with a list of your "don't wants" and write down as much as you can think of. If you were to design your life exactly the way you wanted, what would you get rid of or change? Once you've compiled that list, you'll have a better idea of what you do want. You'll be able to write specific and personal affirmations.

The next mistake that people often make is not saying the affirmations with positive emotions attached. They think that the words themselves hold the power, when in fact it's their own emotions that power the affirmations. You've got to get excited about your affirmations. As you read your affirmations, you've got to be getting more and more thrilled with the idea of having these desires manifest in your life. Affirmations work best when they are:

- Said daily

- Phrased in the present tense

- Phrased using "I am"

- Spoken with positive words, rather than negative

So instead of affirming "I don't want these bills" or "I no longer have a lot of debt", you would affirm "I have plenty of money for all of my needs." Many people resist using affirmations because they can't understand how repeating phrases again and again will change their lives. If you fit into this category, you may not understand how the process of affirmations works. Here's something that may surprise you: You are already using affirmations, whether consciously or not! You have a constant inner monologue running through your mind. You are affirming certain beliefs to yourself every minute of every day. What you may not realise is that the content of these messages is within your control.

Affirmations are a process of deliberately programming your mind to function for you in a specific way. To understand what this means, you need to go back to Chapter IV and look at the stick figure and the sections on your mind. Reprogramming can take place through the use of affirmations. Anything repeated on the conscious level of your mind (like affirmations) will eventually become programmed on the subconscious level. You've already experienced a great deal of programming in your life up to this point. Any attitudes, behaviours, or events that were repeated consistently in your life have programmed your subconscious mind. Repeating positive statements about the changes you want to see in your life will reprogram your subconscious mind. However, it takes time for these new thoughts and beliefs to really take root and grow. That's why you won't see obvious results from affirmations in just a few days. With consistent effort, your new beliefs will sink down into your subconscious mind and become part of your automatic behaviour.

Affirming Gratefully

Too many people use affirmations robotically without really getting a lot out of them. The main reason is lack of emotional involvement in the affirmations. The process of saying affirmations can be disconnected from your emotions almost entirely if you are not careful. This makes them a lot less effective. To change this, you need to cultivate a feeling of gratitude while you say your affirmations. In other words, act as if you have already received whatever you desire. Imagine the power of this! By expressing gratitude for the pay raise or promotion, meeting the love of your life, or achieving the success you desire, you are affirming to the universe that it is already your reality, and you are grateful for it. Being grateful for what you don't yet have will put your emotions on the right level for receiving exactly that.

Your emotional level will then be tied directly to your affirmations. You'll see quicker results and be more confident about the process. Your emotional state during the affirmations process is vital, and gratitude is one of the most powerful emotions. It puts you in a state of receiving and allowing manifestation to happen. You can use gratitude with your affirmations by using statements similar to the following:

- I am so happy and grateful for my beautiful family.

- I am so happy and grateful for our successful business.

- I am so happy and grateful for my optimal health.

These affirmations accomplish two feats. First, they are written in the present tense, which is a requirement for successful affirmations. Affirmations must be written as if the thing you want is already happening or has already happened. You do not say, "I am so happy and grateful because my business is going to be a success." When you use a gratitude affirmation like those above, you are invoking a feeling of already having that which you desire. Secondly, you are putting yourself in a "receiving" emotional state. When you use affirmations similar to the previous examples, you are ready to receive what you desire.

You are signalling to the universe that you are ready and willing to receive. Your expectation of healing, or of a home, a spouse, or a raise, places you in the right frame of heart (not mind!) in order to receive. You can also increase the positive emotions in your life by cultivating an attitude of gratitude outside of your affirmations practice. Many people forget to be grateful because they feel like they have nothing to be grateful for. They're not happy with their financial situations, jobs, relationships, weight, health, cars, homes... and on and on. Know this: No matter what else is happening in your life, there is always something for which you can be grateful.

Being grateful for all that you have around you will make it easier to be in the right frame of mind and heart to make affirmations work for you. Using gratitude as a constant emotional state in your daily life, as well as when you use affirmations, is essential. You'll get more out of your affirmations practice and see results more quickly.

Chapter Questions

1. Write down ten things you can be grateful for right now.

2. Commit to buying a journal to use as a gratitude book, and do so in the next 24 hours. Then commit to writing in it on a daily basis for at least 30 days.

3. Write down five ways in which you can show gratitude on a daily basis.

4. From the list of affirmations in this chapter, select two (or make up your own) and commit to saying them 100 times a day for 30 days.

Chapter X

Soar with Eagles: Take Flight

The sky is one of the most peaceful places I know... you are free...you can fly alongside a wild swan and hear the beat of its wings. You can look into the eyes of an eagle.

— Sir Richard Branson

We began our journey together with the story of the Phoenix. Now, we'd like to end with the fable of the eagle. This story is paramount to our lives and helped us realise that out of adversity comes new opportunity and life.

One of my mentors had me do an exercise to determine my core values. In doing so, I had to find a symbol and a slogan which represented my journey in life and incorporated my core values. After much writing and reflection, I recalled reading about the fable of the eagle. Each time I revisited the story and researched information about the eagle, I became more convinced that I had found my symbol. The slogan just naturally followed: Soar on the winds of freedom.

— Bill

The eagle is a magical bird that can live and prosper for up to 70 years. But to reach this age, the eagle must make a hard decision. Some time after the eagle reaches the age of 40, its long and flexible talons can no longer grab the prey which serves as its food. Its long, sharp beak becomes bent. Its old, heavy wings, due to their thick feathers, become stuck to its chest and make it difficult to fly. The eagle is left with only two options: die, or go through a painful process of change, which lasts 150 days.

The process requires that the eagle fly to a mountain top and sit on its nest. There, the eagle knocks its beak against a rock until the beak is smashed off. After that, the eagle will wait for a new beak to grow back, and then it will pluck out its talons. When its new talons grow back, the eagle will start plucking its old wing feathers. And after five months, the eagle takes its famous flight of rebirth and lives for another 30 years.

Why is change needed? In order to survive, we often have to start a process of change. We sometimes need to get rid of old memories, habits, and other baggage from the past. Only freed from past burdens can we take advantage of the present. The road is never straight and direct. Many times in our life together, we didn't know where our next dollar would come from or how we were going to pay the bills. Looking back, we realise that we attracted and created all of those events which enabled us to work through our own personal issues in our own time. We did what we needed to do to become who we are today, and we are grateful for all that has challenged us in life. We are grateful for the opportunities and obstacles.

Each time we hit the fear barrier, we reminded ourselves to focus on where we were going and what we really wanted. We had to remove our focus from what was going wrong and focus on what we wanted to accomplish. Often, we found ourselves distracted by things that did not move us along in the direction we wanted to go. This was a learned behaviour. We had to learn to stop and ask ourselves what we really wanted. Were we currently doing the most productive thing possible at that moment?

Who are your heroes? What are your ideals? Do you need to change your behaviours, style, or habits to become the person you want to be? Make room for all the good in your life. You have to let go of something in order to get what you want. It's like climbing a ladder. You have to get off the bottom step in order to get to the top. Let go of something of lesser value in order to gain something of higher value. Maybe you have to give up 30 minutes of TV every night. Maybe you have to get up 30 minutes earlier every morning, or say no to some activities that drain your energy from what you want to achieve.

Do you feel you are worthy of success and abundance? If not, you have to focus on being worthy. Welcome success into your life. Being successful can be quite scary. Based on our own paradigms, we had to work on the feeling of being truly worthy of great success and abundance. Sometimes it is hard to give up even the things you don't like because they are familiar. New habits are hard to get but easy to live with. So make sure you focus on getting good new habits. It takes at least 30 days to form a new habit, so be focused.

Our potential is unlimited. Just think about all the things that people have achieved against all odds. Normally, we stop ourselves through our limiting beliefs about our potential and what is possible for us. Thoughts mixed with emotions – desire and high expectations – create a magnetic field around us, pulling towards us the resources, people, and opportunities needed to achieve our goals. This is why it is so important to be emotionally involved in our goals.

You should willingly give and gracefully receive. If you give with your heart, by law it must come back to you. How generous are you with the people around you? Regarding tithing, no matter how you view this idea, it has been said that, "You give with your spade and the universe will give back with its shovel."

Your intellectual faculties will take you from your dreams to your destination. You have to win it in your heart and mind before you can own it in your life. From physics, we know that energy always attracts like energy. Your dream and the solution to achieve it are on the same energy level. So in order to succeed, you must put yourself in the right energy field. The realization that fear is nothing more than a stumbling block is the key to success. To truly face your fear, you must explore the reasons behind it. Identify the basis of your fear. Is it based on the truth, a lie, a feeling, or a past experience?

We have to change our perspectives on fear; otherwise, we become whatever we fear. This happens because our predominant thoughts create our current lives. If we obsess over one particular fear, we are really just reinforcing it in our minds. We become whatever we allow ourselves to mentally dwell upon. Our success with Teggelove Mentoring and Coaching was just a matter of our willingness to face our fears and take action regardless. We all need to conquer fear to really start living the lives we want to live – the lives we deserve. We got where we are today by letting go, moving forward, and being grateful.

We have to ask ourselves who we want to be and what we want to contribute to the world. These are the foundational questions that set your sights on your vision for your life. Your life starts when you begin to practice the principles underlying the truth that you create your own success. Always work on your personal growth, and measure the potential for your life by your vision and not your grades. In the end, what you believe about yourself is what you are going to create in the world. It doesn't really matter how good your grades are in regards to financial success. If you graduate "top of the class", yet you have an underlying belief that you don't deserve to make money, or deep down inside you think that highly successful people are fundamentally bad, you will probably never allow yourself to become financially successful. Even if you do have financial success, you will not feel the personal sense of fulfilment that you deserve. This is fundamental information, but most people never talk about it. Use these years to discover what lies within you. Make the necessary changes in your beliefs that are in alignment and resonation with your life's purpose.

Don't listen to others when it comes to your dreams and your purpose. The only person who can truly appreciate and understand your purpose is you. It is your creation. By the way, not listening to others includes not listening to your own internal negative thoughts. Whatever you choose to do, you must know that you will be growing personally and that you will be contributing to others as you grow your business. What do you bring to this world? You may not know the answer consciously, but you do know within you.

Trust yourself and empower others. We are all unique, and so are our purposes. With all of the successes we've had, a voice within us was telling us we needed to do something else. Throughout the years, many books have inspired us, which is why we've included titbits and lessons from many other authors in this book. So much was explained to us by reading these books that we decided to inspire others with our own book, *Beyond Broke*. This book will take you through your personal barriers so that you can create the life you desire.

We love that we have been a part of something good and that we are able to contribute to the lives of those who need encouragement as well. Now we are grateful that we have the opportunity to help others who are still struggling to discover who they truly are. We all have our own version of what the perfect life would look like. We should all be financially sound, living in the style we choose; we all deserve to be fit and healthy. Mostly, we each deserve and can create fulfilment and joy in our lives. It is our sincere hope and desire that this book will help others find their truths and create the breakthroughs that will help them reshape and redefine their personal and professional lives.

The storm has become our metaphor for our financial crisis. We have learned that the eagle never flees from a storm; rather, it turns to face it head-on. As the storm approaches, the eagle uses the currents of the oncoming winds to lift and carry itself over and beyond to safety and freedom. We too have faced our financial storm head-on and are now flying on winds of freedom.

– Geraldine and Bill

The song "On Winds of Freedom", written and recorded by Geraldine, is available for your listening pleasure and inspiration on her music website www.geraldineteggelove.com.

Chapter Questions

1. If it is time for your personal lift-off, what are three things you are excited about?

2. Rewrite your top five core values. How does money rate?

3. Who will be your mentors and advisors?

4. In relation to your finances, list three action steps you are committed to taking (such as making an appointment with a financial mentor or starting a saving plan). Give yourself a deadline.

Music to Uplift
and Inspire

You have read the book. Now be uplifted and inspired by
songs which each tell a story and impart a message of hope.

Geraldine Teggelove, author and now singer / songwriter,
is living the life of her dreams and wishes to share her
story with you. Many of the songs relate to events and
circumstances surrounding the theme of the book
Beyond Broke.

Be treated to a delightful and moving array of songs and
experiences as Geraldine shares her magnificent talent.
Her voice has a richness embedded in wisdom and life
experience; the quality belies her years.

Two professionally produced CDs are currently available.
As well as singing all vocals, Geraldine has personally
written the music and lyrics for all songs.

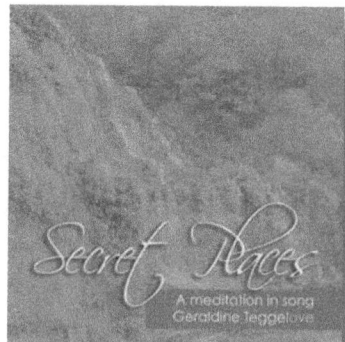

visit
www.geraldineteggelove.com
for information and purchase

Are you ready to change your life for the better?

- Improve your health
- Grow your wealth
- Invigorate your relationships
- Flourish in your career

......and RESTORE BALANCE IN YOUR LIFE.

You've read the book, now take the action!

The alternative?
Insanity: doing the same thing over and over again and expecting different results. —Albert Einstein

The F.L.I.G.H.T Plan Program workshop

is now available to assist you to move on from your financial demise and into a life of prosperity.

visit
www.flightplanprogram.com

for details about our FREE information sessions.

Special 2-for-1 program offer: as a purchaser of this book, receive 2 F.L.I.G.H.T Plan Program workshop tickets for the price of 1. Enter the code FPW010 in shopping basket when registering. See website for further information.

Want to make money from referrals?

Join our affiliate program

In Chapter II of this book, we talked about the many ways in which extra income can be generated. Now, you too can be part of the success of *Beyond Broke* and the programs and resources available through Teggelove Mentoring & Coaching. Build another stream of income for yourself, from home, by participating in this exciting affiliate program.

Visit
www.flightplanprogram.com
for further information and to register.